LIFE AS A MASTERPIECE

Life as a Masterpiece

DESIGN AND LIVE A LIFE
YOU LOVE TODAY

Cathy Christen

LIONCREST
PUBLISHING

LIFE AS A MASTERPIECE
Design and Live a Life You Love Today

ISBN   978-1-5445-1255-6 *Paperback*
       978-1-5445-1256-3 *Ebook*

To my sister Nathalie, who dedicated her time on this earth to pushing her students to think bigger about what was possible for them, and to all the Christen and Vazquez generations to come. May they be inspired to live every day as it could be their last and use up all the gifts they've been given to do the most good on this earth!

"Some of us are given more time on this Earth than others, but none of us should ever take the gift of life for granted. If we strive to be the best we can be, committing ourselves to what is right and true, while helping others along the way, then we will leave our own story worth the telling and be a shining example for our children and our grandchildren and all those great, great, great, great grandchildren in those far off times to come."

LAURENCE OVERTIRE

Contents

Foreword

As an author, keynote speaker, and former life/business coach, I am sold on the belief that regardless of where we are in our lives, we can always take it to the next level. I have dedicated the majority of my adult life to studying human potential and personal development, and helping people take all areas of their life to new levels of success and fulfillment.

I have found that most people have never taken time to really identify exactly what they want their life to look like. They have general ideas...*I want more money...I want to be happier...I know I should be healthier...*However, despite these vague ambitions, most of us just take whatever comes our way and accept it as reality. Sometimes we even attach negative meaning to it, which can make our lives seem insignificant or troubled. We all go through things that may not be ideal, but we all have the ability to decide how we react to them and assign our life experiences any meaning we choose.

As cliché as it may sound, every single one of us deserves to live the life of our dreams, but very few come close. Most people settle for a life of mediocrity, never tapping into our ability to design our lives to be what we want them to be. It's up to us! For over sixteen years, Cathy Christen has been helping young entrepreneurs push past their current reality and create a life that in many cases they weren't aware was even possible for them.

In this book, Cathy does an incredible job empowering and equipping you with tools to design and live your best life. She walks you through exercises to expand your mind on what's truly possible for your life, encourages you to acknowledge and fully utilize the gifts you've been given, reminds you that you do deserve to live the life of your dreams, and inspires you to start now because your days are indeed limited!

With the tools in this book you will:

- Paint a clear vision for what is possible for your life
- Bring a higher sense of purpose to your daily routines
- Learn specific steps to turn your dreams into reality
- Identify and create the best environment for your growth

- Craft daily routines that set you up to win every day
- Be prepared to overcome the obstacles that will come your way

In December of 1999, I was found dead at the scene after a tragic car accident. Although I was very fortunate to be given a second chance at life after six minutes without a heartbeat and six days in a coma, I woke to the news that I might never be able to walk again. At first, I struggled with the question *Why did this happen to me?* but soon understood that focusing on what I wish hadn't happened to me would never get me to where I wanted to be. Since I couldn't change what happened, I made a decision to move forward and dedicate my life to achieving my full potential and achieving my dreams so that I could help others do the same.

I hope it does not take a potential tragedy to push you towards achieving your full potential and living your best life. In this book, you have the tools. It's up to you to make a decision to take action, design a life you love, and start living it today! Reading this book is your first step.

With Love & Gratitude,
—Hal Elrod

Introduction

THE CLOCK IS TICKING

It was a Friday afternoon in 2001 during the summer between my freshman and sophomore years of college. Almost nineteen years old, I was working as a counselor at a sports camp in my hometown. I was driving home, my head full of plans for weekend fun, when a sudden, violent blow sent my car spinning into the middle of the road.

Petrified in my seat, I watched the world race around me in a sickening blur, the freeway median getting closer with each revolution. All I could think was, "Oh my gosh. This is it. I'm about to die."

There was a heart-stopping thud, the sharp sound of metal crunching against concrete, and then everything got very quiet. As white smoke began to billow against the windshield, I sat in the driver's seat frozen, taking in the blinking lights, the inflated airbags, the stillness of my own body. Where was my seatbelt? How did I not have a scratch on me? Could I actually be dead, looking down at my own lifeless body? It didn't seem impossible.

Just in case, though, I decided to get out of the car. There was a lot of smoke coming out now—if I wasn't actually dead, there was no sense in waiting for the car to go up in flames. I opened the door, slid out of the seat, walked across three lanes to the side of the road, and took a seat on the curb, waiting for whatever might happen next.

After a few minutes—or maybe a few hours, who knows—the police pulled up with an ambulance right behind them. They swarmed my car, tugged at the door, and sent somebody back for the jaws of life. I heard them say, "We've got to get whoever's in there out!" I wondered if I was about to see my own lifeless body get pulled out of the vehicle. But once they got the door open, the police found no one inside.

An onlooker got a cop's attention and pointed toward me. "The driver's right over there," he said. "It's that girl. I saw her walk across the street."

The cop and a paramedic made their way across the road to me. "Were you driving that vehicle?" they asked.

I stared back and then abruptly answered, "Yes." That was the first moment it hit me: I was still here. I was alive.

When I told them I was the driver, they bombarded me with questions. How had I gotten out of the car? How did I have no bruises, burns, or seatbelt marks on my body? When I told them that I'd just opened the door and walked out, they shook their heads in disbelief. It made no sense. It was impossible.

One of the cops looked me dead in the eye. His face was pale, like he'd seen a ghost. "Young lady," he said, "I don't know who you are, and I don't know what just happened. But something kept you here, and you'd better do something with that."

I went through the rest of that day in a daze. I felt it in my heart that he was right. Something supernatural had intervened to keep me not only alive, but also completely unharmed. But why? What purpose did I have that made my life worth saving in this unbelievable way?

To say this accident was a wake-up call would be an understatement. Like most young people my age, I lived as though I had all the time in the world. I worked hard in school, taking steps toward getting a job and becoming an adult. But my real focus was on having a good time, running around with my friends, and not getting caught when I got into mischief.

I had no idea how much this accident would shape the rest of my life. It seemed like a small piece of the puzzle, but it was the piece that would help everything else come together. I realized that life was incredibly short. *I could have died today*, I thought to myself, *and I could just as easily be gone tomorrow*. I heard a voice in my head, echoing the cop's words: "You were kept here for a reason," it said, "so you'd better do something with it."

I didn't know yet what I was called to do, but I knew that I was called to do more. I felt a higher sense of purpose and realized that my life could have more meaning if I chose to step up and see how grand it could be. Who could I impact? Who could I inspire to maximize the days they were given? What legacy would I leave behind? These questions began haunting my thoughts and actions.

CALLED TO MORE

There's nothing like growing up as part of a family of six living in a two-bedroom apartment to give you a drive to succeed. I saw doing well in school as the key to a life in which I'd never have to struggle financially. This drive, combined with my being a quick learner, made it easy for me to get straight A's while still being able to party with my friends.

Before the accident, I'd felt like it was okay to be a little irresponsible. I'd assumed I had plenty of time to do all the things I wanted to in my life. But this new sense of a higher calling lit a fire under my butt. I started putting more effort into school than I ever had before. I went back to church and threw myself into helping others. I also began examining my talents and gifts to see how I might use them to not only design and live my best life, but to also help others live theirs. What could I do that I would really enjoy and that would also utilize my strengths? I knew from being the eldest of four kids, captain of school athletics, and president of most clubs I was a part of, that I was a strong leader. I also knew from an early age I had a good head for business, and that I had great people skills. My dad always said I could sell ice to an Eskimo.

During childhood Easter egg hunts, I would find the silent eggs and switch them for noisy eggs, knowing the noisy ones had change and the silent ones had dollar bills. I would also offer my younger siblings the opportunity to have *five* pennies in exchange for their *one* quarter. ("Wouldn't you prefer to have five of something?") I am embarrassed to say that, but give me a little grace—I was six years old!

As I searched for a more meaningful summer job summer of 2002, I knew I wanted to do something that would hone my personal sales, business, and leadership skills. Regardless of what I would do in the future, I knew I would always be selling an idea, service, product or myself. One day, as I was walking through the school parking lot, headed for the library to job search, I noticed a business card lying on the pavement. It said, "Student work. Entry level sales/service. Meaningful job experience. Resume builder. Scholarships offered." I thought, "Hey, I need all those things!" That card led me to Vector Marketing. And what began as a fast-paced summer job at that company ultimately became what expanded my entire vision of what was possible in my life and for others. The formative years I spent with Vector/Cutco showed me I could achieve far more than I'd been able to imagine.

THE TIME IS NOW

As this transformation was happening to me, I began to see myself through a new lens, and couldn't help but start seeing my friends through the same one. Wanting them to experience the same sense of purpose I did, I urged them to stop wasting their days smoking weed and playing video games. They said they were just having fun, but all I could see was their amazing potential being wasted.

During the next several months, my group of friends

changed, particularly as I put in more time with my work community. The people I met at Vector were serious about moving forward in life. They aimed to accomplish things I'd never even thought about, such as building wealth and owning and running their own businesses. Being around people with these big goals challenged me to think bigger. I realized that anyone could achieve greatness, regardless of how limited their resources were. In fact, the people who worked harder appreciated their lives more than those who had everything handed to them, because they never took it for granted.

I didn't have a wealthy family or amazing connections who could pave my way to success. But I had a great attitude, a great support system, a great work ethic, and a determination to find (or create) each next step that would get me up the ladder. I believed my manager when he told me that if you have a great attitude and you're willing to work hard for what you want, you can make anything happen in life. I saw that no matter where I wanted to go, all I had to do was make a plan to get there, and then put that plan into action.

Before my car accident, the only real goal I'd had for my life was to not be broke. But now, I started seeing goals as the key to any opportunity I wanted. I could build and run a business of my own. I could coach people to find tools and resources to create a life they loved. I could give to others and make a real impact in the world.

I didn't know how long my chapter in this world would last, but I knew that I wanted to do the most with it that I could. There was no time to wait. The time to make my mark was now.

COMMON PROBLEMS, UNCOMMON TOOLS

After over a decade of coaching young entrepreneurs and people who are struggling with the transition into the "real" world, I've observed four common problems:

- First, many people simply don't realize what they're capable of. They have incredible gifts, but no one has ever challenged them to think about how they could use those gifts to serve at a higher level. They live in the reality of what is, instead of feeling empowered to create whatever reality they want.
- Second, I've found that many young people think the way I used to: that they have plenty of time. They're not motivated to take life as serious now, and they feel no real urgency to work on their goals. Years later, these people wake up, realize none of their dreams ever came true, and feel like failures. They knew what they were capable of, but they spent their best years wasting their potential. Now, they feel like it's too late to get started. (Even when it's not!)
- Third, some people are just angry at the world. They feel that they've been dealt a bad hand in life—a loss,

a handicap, being born into a certain kind of family or economic situation. They're bitter and frustrated because they don't have it as easy as other people seem to, and they use this bitterness as an excuse for never working on their goals. They don't realize how much power there is in owning their story and their unique struggles, and in using these as fuel for achieving their dreams.

- Finally, I find that a lot of people simply lack confidence. Sometimes they've been abused, verbally or physically; other times, they've been programmed through things people have told them all their lives. That they were stupid or ugly. That they weren't capable of things, always messed things up, and would never amount to anything. Those messages stuck in their heads, making them scared to take a step forward, because they were convinced they couldn't succeed, and the last thing they wanted to do was prove their naysayers right. What these individuals don't realize is that failure plays a part in all the greatest achievements. The most influential figures in modern culture—business leaders, innovators, impactors—all understand that failing is part of the success process. Every failure can both teach you something and make you stronger, if you allow it to.

The good news is that these problems don't have to hold you back.

This book is designed to help you realize that you can achieve more than you can imagine. It's intended to help you set goals for creating a life you love and give you the tools to achieve those goals, regardless of how limited your resources might be. Most of all, it's designed to help you understand that your days are limited, which means it's time to start NOW!

I know these tools will work for you because they've worked for me and thousands of others. Using the principles and guidelines in this book, I went from being an inexperienced nineteen-year-old college student from a lower-middle-class background to earning a six-figure income by my mid-twenties. My husband and I have used the tools in this book to build an incredible life that we love. We can spend time with our loved ones, knock three to five dream trips off our bucket list every year, offer financial help to family members when they need it, support missions around the world, and save for our future goals without ever having to worry about money. This life may not be everyone's ideal picture, but it's the one we dreamed of for years, and I can tell you that it's pretty awesome getting to live it.

Along with all the personal rewards my husband and I enjoy, I've created the kind of professional life the nineteen-year-old me would never have dreamed was possible. I used to wake up every day super stressed, wondering, *Am I going to have enough? How hard will I have to work to take care of my family? Will I be able to go on vacation and see the world, or will I have to struggle?* But by using the tools in this book, I developed a strong direct sales business that essentially runs itself, co-founded a health and wellness company, and then branched out into a coaching business that takes me all over the country, running events that impact people's lives for the better. I've used my gifts, skills, and interests to create financial freedom for myself while loving the life I live. I wake up every morning with peace in my heart, knowing that I'm going to have everything I ever wanted—and more, if I want it. The anxiety is gone; I feel centered, empowered, and excited; I know that if I put in the work, things will come together.

This is what I want for you. No matter what your goals are, no matter where you're starting from, I know you can move forward. The tools and resources in this book will take you from wherever you are today to wherever you want to be.

It's okay if you don't know exactly what your purpose is yet. I believe our purpose in life should be to find the things that make us come fully alive, and live that out at the highest level! If you feel there is a bigger purpose calling you forward, you're ready to get started. Your life is too precious to waste another minute. The clock is ticking, so let's get started.

PART ONE

Your Vision

Create the grandest vision for your life possible...You become what you believe.

OPRAH WINFREY

CHAPTER 1

What's Possible?

There is no man living who isn't capable of doing more than he thinks he can do.

HENRY FORD

I was managing the Ft. Lauderdale, Florida, office of Vector Marketing when Tyler showed up for his first interview in December 2005. He was seventeen years old, and you could see he was a little rough around the edges. He'd been expelled from two high schools and had many clashes with authority. His parents had kicked him out of the house, worried about the bad example he was setting for his younger siblings. The previous year, he'd spent time in juvenile prison for selling illegal substances.

Despite all this, Tyler had been recommended by one of our former employees. He'd assured me Tyler was a good kid and just needed an opportunity to put his strengths and talents toward something good. Few people were willing to give Tyler that opportunity, on account of his past. But Tyler was the real deal, the former employee assured me. He was smart, had great people skills, and was capable of doing incredible work.

I could believe it. As we talked, I sensed something special about Tyler. Not only was he well-spoken and personable, but he also had a certain spark that made him stand out from other interviewees. Even though I'd just met this kid, I already believed in him. I made it my mission to establish a connection with Tyler. In the two weeks between his hiring and start date, I sent him a Christmas card and said I looked forward to seeing him in training. He told me later that he'd been having doubts about the job, but the card gave him the extra nudge he needed to show up.

MORE THAN A STATISTIC

I was sure from the get-go that Tyler would succeed, but I never imagined how well he'd do. Shortly after he completed training, Tyler sold over $10,000 of product (highest level of commissions for an entry-level representative) in the span of a week, a figure that barely one percent of Cutco sales reps ever achieve. Talk about impressive.

Tyler didn't slow down, either. He continued to work

incredibly hard, exceeding everyone's expectations. Eventually, I asked Tyler if he'd ever thought about applying for one of the company's management internships. For Tyler, it was ironic to even consider a leadership position, given his past troubles with authority. Whatever anyone had told him to do—at home, at school, at church, in society—he'd wanted to do the opposite.

But after hearing me suggest that he had leadership potential, Tyler's mindset began to shift. He realized that being an authority doesn't have to mean being a dictator or talking down to people. Instead, he could motivate people by simply getting to know them, setting a great example for them, and inspiring them to discover their potential. He was in the perfect place to learn for himself that he could, in fact, be a great leader.

Just two months after starting with the company, Tyler was promoted to assistant manager. By the next summer, he was our top assistant manager and the number one team builder in the nation. Tyler kept moving up in our leadership academy until a year later, when he was given the chance to run his own office for the summer.

Throughout his life, Tyler had been judged by so many people. Throughout his childhood, Tyler was always sidelined. No one expected much from him, which made him stop caring about himself. Years of being compared to his "perfect" sister, a straight-A student who never got into trouble, made him feel like a failure. With no one on his side, he had nowhere to go when life got hard. He would respond impulsively and end up doing stupid things that hurt him later.

They thought of him as an inevitable statistic, just another high school dropout who was destined for a bad path. As it turned out, though, Tyler was aware of his potential. All he needed was to get into the right environment.

ENVIRONMENT IS EVERYTHING

Think of a person like a seed. If you leave a seed on the countertop, it will stay the way it is—tiny, hard, and barely noticeable until it rots away. But if you put a seed into the right environment and give it proper nourishment, it can grow into something big, beautiful, and strong, providing oxygen, food, and shelter for everyone around it.

Knowing this, I was intentional about creating an environment where Tyler could grow and see what was truly possible for his life; an environment that would help Tyler learn on his own terms. As it turned out, despite his past reputation as a bad student in high school, he was an eager, hands-on learner, taking loads of notes and engaging readily in discussion. It was easy to see that the classroom setting hadn't brought out the best in him—he had a ton of restless energy and needed to walk around the room or step outside every few minutes. Rather than force him to sit in one place, I told him to do his thing. If being in motion was a better way for him to learn, I was all for it.

One of the biggest lessons Tyler learned was how to handle adversity. As he developed skills for embracing challenges and meeting them head-on, he gained professionalism, self-discipline, and belief in his own potential. He developed leadership and public speaking skills and started working with all types of people.

Tyler even appreciated being pushed by his team to think bigger and never accept anything but his best. This drove him to adopt higher standards for himself, a mindset that caused his success to grow by leaps and bounds. He became so skilled that he even gave back to me. In 2008, we joined forces to help me develop a new sales territory. That summer, Tyler and I made company history. We set the record for the best district office annual performance and broke the all-time summer sales record. A decade later, that record still stands. Better still, we were able to impact so many people, seeing them grow through finding their focus and passion. For me, the best part was seeing Tyler give back so much of what he had gained over the years.

Tyler told me later that I'd changed his life. That felt great to hear, but all I'd really done was help create the conditions that allowed him to grow and thrive. The potential, the hard work, the determination, and the success were all his own.

A LESSON IN ACCOUNTABILITY

I knew Tyler didn't want to be seen as another statistic and wanted to achieve great things. But I also knew that his success depended on him not just thinking about his goals but finding accountability for them. As we worked together, I helped him to consider every choice he made in relation to his goals. Would it get him closer to being financially stable? Would it give him the skills he needed to get any job? Would it get him closer to the kind of success he wanted? Whenever he was lacking motivation, I'd remind him of what he wanted to achieve. Did he want to show his family that he wasn't a failure and could be a great example? Tyler had been given a great opportunity, and I wasn't about to let him get off track and waste it.

Don't get me wrong, I wasn't holding a stick over him. I was simply reminding him of the life he wanted. The choice to achieve it was up to him.

Like Tyler, you also have unlocked potential waiting inside of you. Wondering if you have what it takes to succeed is just a distraction; the real question is whether you'll choose to harness your potential and find a way to make the most of it.

UNLOCK YOUR POTENTIAL

Today, Tyler is married, lives in his dream home, and runs his own company. Everyone who knew him as a teenager is in awe of his success, his parents most of all. They couldn't believe how hard he worked, how focused he was, how much he achieved. Every morning, he'd be ready for work at seven o'clock, regardless of what he'd done the night before. The son they'd always thought of as lazy and rebellious had a real motivation to succeed.

I can still remember being at his wedding in 2013, when his mom came up to hug me, tears welling up in her eyes. She always knew how great her son could be, but never knew how to get that greatness out of him. Like a lot of parents out there, she believed that kids need to go to school in order to achieve greatness. What she didn't realize was that Tyler wasn't wired that way. School wasn't the best environment for him.

That's not to say that school isn't for anyone. Personally, I was a straight-A student in high school, valedictorian of my senior class, and graduated with a 3.9 GPA from my university's honors program. School is an incredible environment to help many people grow and develop, but it's not for everyone—some people's paths don't require that traditional route. What *is* vital is to find the environment that taps into your potential and brings out your best.

IT'S TIME TO DREAM AGAIN

When I was little, I really wanted to fly. I was convinced that if I tried hard enough and got a good enough running start, I could fly right off the ground just like a bird. When you're a kid, there's no limit to the ideas you have or your belief that you can achieve them. However, once we grow up, people are quick to point out everything that's unrealistic about our goals. Of course, my physical body on its own would never be able to fly, but there are now so many ways we are able to soar through the air. Dreams like I had in my youth create space for innovation and incredible breakthroughs.

If people don't crush your childhood dreams, circumstances often will. A lot of people stop dreaming once they start thinking realistically about money. I've met so many talented and creative people—writers, artists, musicians, experts in every field imaginable—who have been discouraged from using their incredible talents by the day-to-day necessity of supporting themselves or taking care of a family. Whenever they start to dream again, they're told to forget it and focus on a "real" job.

This is why so many people go through life like robots, not

taking advantage of their strengths and losing all connection with the things that make them happiest. They spend day after day rushing, stressing, worrying, picking up the kids, cooking dinner, and getting barely enough sleep until a few decades later, when they look back and ask themselves where their lives went.

START BY IDENTIFYING YOUR STRENGTHS

This isn't always as easy as it sounds. Like a lot of people, you may have been taught to downplay your strengths and abilities to avoid sounding arrogant. But to become the best version of yourself, you have to own and take pride in the talents you already possess. Ready? Let's do it.

Start by asking yourself what you're great at. You might be a great problem solver or listener. You might be very good at presenting and connecting with people, or your strengths might lie with data and numbers. You could be super creative. Think about all the positive attributes you have, and write these down. Think about qualities that friends have complimented you for. Think about tasks that have gotten you noticed by your boss. Think about the things that nobody else might have seen but that made you feel proud when you did them. Even if you don't consider an attribute a big deal, jot it down anyway. It's probably a bigger deal than you think.

Pause + Reflect

Take a second right now and list some of your
gifts, talents, and strengths. Don't be shy!

Look at your list and ask yourself how often you use those
strengths. Which ones are a part of your everyday life?
Do you demonstrate your strengths enough for other
people to know about them? If you want to move forward and achieve success, you need to start by utilizing
your gifts.

If you don't do the things that make you come alive,
you're not truly living. In contrast, the more you come
alive, the more others around you will come alive. Furthermore, the more you use what you already have, the
more the universe will give you. (We'll talk more about
this in chapters 9 and 10.)

While it's definitely important to take responsibility for
your life and the people who depend on you, it's not an

all-or-nothing. There *is* a way to be responsible while incorporating the things that make you come alive.

A great example is my friend Betsy Crouch, whom I initially met at Vector. She and her business partner Zoe at ImprovHQ met while practicing improv for the stage. Today, they lead improv-based workshops with Google, Twitter, and other top IT companies in Silicon Valley and all over the world. They have found a way to use an art form they love to teach invaluable skills—flexibility, quick thinking, problem solving, creativity under pressure—to facilitate growth and change in people's lives and organizations.

In today's society, we beat ourselves up too much...and where does that get us? Take a risk and try giving yourself a pat on the shoulder instead. If you want to attract and create greatness in your life, you need to start focusing on the good. Instead of thinking about your problems or what you lack in life, ask yourself how you can grow with the resources, gifts, and talents that are already available to you. If you sit there and wish you had everything you don't, you'll get nowhere.

When you set a goal for yourself, use what you have to get to where you want to be quicker, rather than sitting around wishing to be where someone else is, or wishing you had their gifts or talents. Your strengths, talents, and attributes were given to you for a reason, and you can do something great with them—something that makes you happy today, versus waiting to accomplish X, Y, and Z before you're happy. The key is figuring out what gives your life joy and meaning, and utilizes the tools you already have within you! I want you to be happy and love the life you're living now.

Pause + Reflect

Kids barely ever stop dreaming, while adults barely stop to dream. If you want more for your life than what you see in it right now, you have to expand your vision of what's possible. The people who move forward in life and move the world forward with them are the people who think bigger.

Think back to when you were a kid and it felt like anything was possible. What did you dream of doing or becoming back then? Now look at your life today through that same lens. If there were no limits standing in your way—no obstacles of time, money or resources—what would you do? Where would you spend your time?

LOOK BEYOND WHAT ALREADY EXISTS

Every time I am on a plane, I am blown away by how a person could possibly conceive of inventing a big piece of metal that could fly people through the air. The complicated mechanics of airplane flight are mind-boggling enough, but what really inspires me is that someone thought that big, and made it happen. I feel the same amazement about all the breakthroughs in science and technology that we see year after year. I love meeting and hearing stories about people who think outside the box—it inspires me to think, "If someone else has done it, then so can I."

If you want to accomplish great things and live your best life, stop looking at what you've already done. Recognize that in order to perform and achieve at your highest level, you can't be realistic and measure your actions solely against your past experiences. After all, if people took action based only on their assessments of what they believed was "realistic" for them to achieve, there wouldn't be much advancement in the world. What is "realistic" is defined by things that have already been done. Imagine if our whole world operated based on what people thought was "realistic."

Shift your thinking to first consider what's possible, and then think about how to get there. That's how companies like Apple and Tesla have become so successful. Imagine back in the day when the lightbulb was invented. There must have been so many people who thought the idea was crazy. The most successful people are not only the ones who have the crazy ideas, but the ones who find out how to make those ideas a reality.

DO SOMETHING TODAY

People put a lot of pressure on themselves to figure out their purpose in life. Let me make it a little easier for you: find a purpose that aligns with your values and brings you joy, a purpose that makes your soul smile! Then decide to live intentionally in alignment with it. When you do this, you become a light that shines bright for everyone else.

Pause + Reflect

Stop to capture some of the things that bring you the most joy, happiness, or fulfillment. We could add so much more joy to our lives by identifying things that make us smile and doing more of them! What brings you to life? What truly makes you happy, inspired, full of energy? What could you do all day and happily wake up at 5 a.m. to do all over again?

The purpose that makes each person shine bright will be different for everyone. My dad always felt his purpose in life was to be an amazing husband and father; to create an incredible family. All he ever wanted in life was to have kids, and when he's around his family, you can see him come alive. My dad shines so bright in his little part of the world, and everyone around him loves to be around it.

However, you don't have to know what your purpose is to start living a life you love right now. What really counts is finding ways to recover the joy in your life. If singing, dancing, and acting make you come alive, make time for those activities by joining a local music group or signing up for a dance class. Organize a fun date with your partner or spouse once a week, and do something that makes you both laugh and smile. Incorporate fun team-building activities at work that make people laugh and build stronger bonds between co-workers.

A great example of this is Epic Freight Solutions, a company that has been voted one of the top places to work for years in the Los Angeles area. They have themed Mondays where people of all ages dress up for work (superhero day, crazy hat day, '70s day, etc.). They hold push-up contests in the middle of the work day. They are masters in the "art" of recognition and making people feel great!

SEE IT FOR YOURSELF

You can create anything you want to, as long as you actualize it in your head. Challenge yourself to picture it. One of my favorite sayings is: *If you can see it, you can achieve it.* The first step is to see an idea in your head. The next is to figure out how to get it done.

Design Exercise

Take a moment to close your eyes and visualize your ideal life right now. What does living a life you love look like? What are you doing professionally, personally, for others, and for yourself? Describe as detailed as possible:

CHAPTER 2

What Do You Want?

People are unique in their ability to imagine a more abundant future.

MATTHEW KELLY

I didn't know what to expect when Matthew Kelly, motivational speaker and author of books like *Rhythm of Life, Seven Levels of Intimacy*, and *The Dream Manager* took the stage at the sales leadership conference I attended in 2006. But as soon as he opened his mouth, the audience of hundreds drifted away—it felt like there was nobody in the room but Matthew and me. His words brought something beyond the self-empowering, goal-based message that had driven me forward to that point in my life.

Matthew told a story from his book *The Dream Manager* about a janitorial company that, despite the menial nature of the tasks its employees were hired to do, was a place where people lined up to apply for jobs. The company had a magnetic environment that stemmed from a very specific module in their employee training: the dream session.

Normally, when someone applies for a job to mop floors and clean toilets, no one really asks them what their bigger dreams are. Employers simply assume the applicant is trying to make ends meet. But this company brought in a "Dream Manager" who would sit down with employees and talk to them about their bigger purpose behind their job. What were they working toward, on a personal level? What was their plan for their life, and how did they see this job contributing to it?

Matthew said that regardless of what somebody does for a living, what makes them feel fulfilled is the meaning behind their work. When employees at this company began consciously connecting their work to bigger goals like buying a house or sending a kid to college, their experience and performance were transformed.

These words shone a spotlight on my own thoughts and habits around work. I realized that while I had always been determined to avoid what I didn't want (e.g., struggling with money the way my family always had), I had never thought deeply about what I *did* want out of life. Not having a clear goal that called me forward had influenced my life direction and my sense of identity. I knew I could do well in school and in my job, take care of myself and my home, carry out the basic tasks in being an adult, but I never really thought I could do *anything* I really wanted to do. I definitely felt there were many more limitations than there actually were.

I heard other people doing things that, to me, sounded almost impossible—traveling the world, having a job you could do from anywhere, owning multiple homes, or going on wild adventures like an African safari or staying on a water hut in the middle of paradise. In my head, these weren't normal things to do, at least not for someone like me who wasn't born with those types of privileges. But Matthew said that when you had a clear vision for what you wanted out of life, you had the beginning of a path to get there. By identifying specific goals and writing them down, your subconscious would immediately begin moving your life in the direction you wanted to go.

TWELVE CATEGORIES

During his talk, Matthew told everyone in the audience to pull out a piece of paper and a pen. He was about to walk us through one of his dream sessions, which included twelve different categories for identifying potential goals.

In preparation for this exercise, he spoke about the

power of writing things down and having clarity in what you wanted. He referenced a famous Harvard study[1] that asked students in that year's graduating class a single question:

Have you set written goals and created a plan for their attainment?

The study showed that 84 percent of the entire class had set no goals at all, while 13 percent of the class had set written goals but had no concrete plans. Just 3 percent of the class had both written goals and concrete plans for how to achieve them after graduation.

Ten years later, the study caught up with those students to survey their progress in life. The 13 percent of the class that had written down their goals but not created plans were making twice as much money as the 84 percent that had set no goals at all. Meanwhile, the 3 percent of the class that had both written goals and a plan were making ten times as much money as the rest of the 97 percent of the class.

I had heard about this study much earlier while pursuing my sales goals, but I had never applied it to other areas of my life. I assumed maybe we'd get down one or two goals

---

1   McCormack, Mark. "What They Don't Teach You at Harvard Business School." http://www.lifemastering.com/en/harvard_school.html

per category, until Matthew announced we wouldn't stop until we wrote down 100 goals.

I looked around to see if anyone else thought that sounded as crazy as it did to me. But as the dream session went on, and I saw my goals multiplying on the paper, I started to feel more confident that anything was possible.

To get us started, Matthew went on to give us thought joggers in the following twelve categories:

CATEGORY #1: PHYSICAL

- How do you want to look and feel in your body?
- Do you want to lose or gain weight? Build muscle or flexibility? Improve your overall health?
- Do you want to sleep more? Drink less? Eat better?
- Do you want to learn a new skill or sport, or accomplish an athletic milestone?

CATEGORY #2: EMOTIONAL

- What things would fill your emotional cup?
- Do you want to find a great relationship, or improve the one you have?
- Do you want to spend more quality time with your kids?
- Do you want to do something special for a friend, loved one, or for yourself?

- Do you want to simply find a sense of contentment and security with who you are?

CATEGORY #3: INTELLECTUAL

- What would stimulate your mind?
- Do you want to learn another language?
- Do you want to return to school to complete an undergraduate or graduate degree?
- Would you like to read a certain number of books this year?

CATEGORY #4: SPIRITUAL

- What would give you greater spiritual fulfillment?
- Would you like to join a local faith community?
- Would you like to begin practicing meditation, mindfulness, or prayer?
- Would you simply like to find some inner peace amid life's uncertainty?

CATEGORY #5: PSYCHOLOGICAL

- What would enhance your mental health and well-being?
- Are you battling with an addiction that you'd like to overcome?
- Would you like to deal with anxiety or depression?

- Would you like to strengthen your psychological will-power in the face of adversity?

CATEGORY #6: MATERIAL

- What kinds of material possessions would give you true, lasting fulfillment?
- Do you want to own a different home, or more than one home?
- Do you want to drive a fancy car?
- Do you want to enjoy more spectacular experiences, such as going to landmark concerts or eating at five-star restaurants?
- Do you want to own a boat, a helicopter, a private jet?

Matthew joked that *Category #6: Material* would be an easy one, given that most of us hold onto a number of highly specific material dreams and goals. The important thing, Matthew said, was to write down material goals that were more than status symbols that were likely to impress other people. Our material goals needed to be things that genuinely satisfied something in our souls.

CATEGORY #7: ADVENTURE

- Do you want to go on a big vacation or make travel a regular part of your life?
- Where would you like to travel?

- What cool experiences would you like to have? (Examples: climb a mountain, go bungee-jumping, ride a motorcycle down the Pacific Coast Highway, skydive in New Zealand, ride a hot air balloon during sunrise in Turkey, etc.)
- What concerts would you like to see?
- What historical monuments would you like to visit?

As I scribbled down my dreams during this exercise, I realized at least half of them related not to things, but to experiences. I found myself writing down "visit the Holy Land," "ride a camel near the pyramids of Egypt," "rent a boat to take around the Fijian Islands," "eat sushi in Japan," "ride an elephant in Thailand," and many other world travel experiences. As much as I'd always believed these experiences weren't realistic for someone like me, it turned out they were things I wanted, and I have been blessed to achieve many since then.

CATEGORY #8: PROFESSIONAL

- What would make you happy in your career or professional life?
- Do you want to earn a certain salary?
- Do you want to get a promotion or rise to a certain position?
- Do you want to do something that improves your company, such as setting up a new training program or building a dynamic team culture?

- Do you want to invent something or start a business of your own?

CATEGORY #9: FINANCIAL

- Do you want to make a certain amount of money per year?
- Do you want to pay off a debt?
- Do you want to be able to donate more to charitable organizations?
- Do you want to be able to support a friend or loved one financially?

For a lot of people—myself in my early years included—setting specific financial goals can seem taboo. After all, nobody wants to think of themselves as being obsessed with money. But Matthew insisted that our dreams about the kind of financial situations we wanted to create for ourselves were just as valid as any other kind of dream we might have. Getting out of debt was a great place to start, he said, but we shouldn't be afraid to dream about, say, having a million dollars in the bank.

I remember thinking, "One day, I want to be in a financial position to give away $100,000 in a year." Now I train those just starting to build wealth to set a goal for when they'll earn their first $100,000, when they'll save their first $100,000, how soon they'll donate their first $100,000, and so on. One of the financial goals I have added on to my Dreams List is to be able to give away $1,000,000 in a year! I can't wait to be able to cross that off. I heard Jeff Hoffman, co-founder and CEO of Priceline.com, once say, "Your success is someone else's miracle," and I can't wait to see the lives our family will impact.

CATEGORY #10: CREATIVE

- What would stimulate your senses of artistry and beauty?
- Do you want to write a novel or a screenplay?
- Do you want to learn a new skill (dance, music, art, etc.) or build on a skill that you already possess but have not put to use in some time?
- Do you want to spend more time enjoying the creativity of others (e.g., visiting museums and galleries, or going to concerts or plays)?
- Do you want to expand your horizons by learning to appreciate art in new ways?

CATEGORY #11: LEGACY

- What kinds of values do you want to pass on to those who come after you?
- Do you want to support more charitable causes?
- Do you want to donate your time to missions or organizations you believe in?
- Do you want to set up an organization that enriches other people's lives?
- Do you want to "pay it forward" by educating others in the skills and knowledge that have made a difference in your own life?

In creating legacy-related goals, Matthew encouraged us to consider how our most important values might translate into action. I had a great point of reference for this category. Throughout my childhood, my parents would always take us on volunteering missions, including serving at soup kitchens and activities at our local church. They had created a legacy of selflessness for our family, training us to work hard and give back, and I realized that was a legacy I wanted to leave behind as well. Along with loving God and serving the needy, I realized that my legacy-dreams also had to do with helping others learn to create a life they love. The desire to help others in this way is a mission that is constantly on my heart. When I realized empowering others in this way could be part of my legacy, I got really excited to think bigger about what I could do with this passion of mine.

CATEGORY #12: CHARACTER

- How would you want someone else to describe your attributes when you aren't around?
- Do you want to be known as a hard worker and a reliable provider for your family?
- Do you want people to remember you with respect and admiration?
- Do you want your friends to remember you as a good listener? A fun and adventurous spirit? Someone who was always there to help when they needed it?
- Do you want people to remember you as someone who inspired them in a certain way?

Dreams List:

2013

have a healthy loving open relationship / marriage - no secrets
Raise 3-5 children
Become a millionaire in a decade
learn to invest
sky dive in Switzerland / new zeland
convertible drive across Tuscany
visit friends in Brazil
safari in South Africa
waterfalls in Zimbabwe
tour the French Riviera
explore Dubai
visit Amange's family in Sweden
Denmark
Norway
Ride an elephant in Thailand
Great Barrier reef in Australia
Live in New Zeland for a mon...
eat Sushi in Japan
go to the Philippines
walk great Wall of China
air balloon ride in Turkey!
Crazy church in Moscow
Water hut in Fiji
margarita in Venezuela
own a property on ...
walking distance ...

37 ... on beach in Barcelona, Sp...
28 week in Highlands N. Scotland
29 roadtrip from San Diego to Vancou...
30 USA RV roadtrip w/ family (my husb...
31 Timeshare / house in Puerto Rico for fa...
32 learn to play guitar
33 learn to play piano
34 take lessons / vocal coaching → SING AGAIN
35 learn to play tennis
36 learn to play golf
37 personal trainer @ my place 4 ...
37 live in help - laundry, cleaning, etc
38 homeschool my kids - involve in all extr...
    curriculars : arts, sports, volunteer...
38 service / mission project annually
    eventually w/ spouse & kids
39 join a boat club - weekends on boat w/ fam...
40 Read 3-4 books annually - minimum for self improvemt
41 wknd getaway annually - conference or pe...
    quiet time, dream session / reflection
43 annual girls getaway - besties & sister
44 weekly date night - mini honeymoon
45 once a month - fancy brunch
46 Parasailing
47 annual family vaca w/ pops ...
    the who...

See U2 in concert
see Marc Anthony live
go to Broadway / live broadway show 3:30-4:30
attend Pilates class w/ ...
Daniel passes to theme park
1 & a memorable week a week a month & make ...
... her that she stays to yourself for
New Year's in Time Square
attend Rockers Christmas show
travel around the world for Christmas
week or more trip to London
one monthly - travel & pampering
Inspect / follow people individually
travel around the world for X months every...
learn to tango!!

41 spend a week in Hana,
5 take salsa classes
51 compete in salsa comp...
52 take Grandma Raquel to C...
53 bridesmaid @ Michelle's wedding
7 see my brother get married
55 visit a nutricionist annually
56 grow herbs / fresh fruits / veggies in bac...
57 love how my body looks.
8 be at 15% body fat
59 stay toned
60 be athletic / join league
61 learn to swim competently
62 run a half marathon annually
63 Run a marathon
64 do a triathalon one day
65 Run 3 miles - 4x a week consistent.
66 be comfortable / confident riding a b...
67 get laser hair removal
68 find a church I love & get involved
69 be able to do a handstand
70 become a certified yoga instructor
71 open a family biz - lunch spot
72 help dad be financially free - no stress
73 become a consistant journaler
74 create 5+ healthy dressings

new recipe 8...
n island - enso...
to be prepping / cooking
showers!!
...rors / lights / comfy seat...

19 ... closet
80 huge ... closet
81 weekly massage @ mi casa
82 peel w/ Palm Trees.
83 lounge area outside / backyard.
84 porch wrap around ? depending are...
85 getaway cabin / ski
86 live w/ no shame
87 inner peace
88 connected to God w/ no guilt
89 forgive myself for bad decisions
90 be a great role model - not just on ou...
91 impeccable word / honesty
92 be trusting of others
93 don't steal joy out of situations
    expecting the worse to happe...
94 enjoy each moment
95 plan on a long life - think ahead ...
96 expect the best from people / inte...
97 celebrate every new decade of lo...
98 find someone I can open up to / s...
99 huge anniversary parties every decade
100 50 yr anniversary ...

THE GPS TO YOUR FUTURE

Throughout this process of walking through the dream session, I felt as though Matthew was giving me permission to embark on something extraordinary. Before the conference, I had always felt like I was moving forward in some capacity—working toward my degree, advancing in my career, improving my life in little ways. What I hadn't realized was that I wasn't moving as quickly as I'd thought. My energy was channeled all over the place because I'd never identified a specific direction for it. Matthew showed me that by connecting to what I truly wanted— no matter how outside the "normal" it seemed—I could create possibilities for myself and make them reality.

For someone who grew up with very little (or as my dad would say, "just enough") and believed that was just the way life was for people like us, the idea of dreaming can sound wishy-washy and too pie-in-the-sky to be practical. But once I put Matthew Kelly's training into practice, I discovered that dreaming is more like putting an address into a GPS and pressing "Start." Specific, intentional dreaming is key to moving your life in a specific, intentional direction. Once I identified where I wanted to go, I suddenly knew what I had to do to get there. And because my GPS knew where it needed to go, each decision I made took me closer to my destination. If something took me in the wrong direction, I was able to reroute and get back on track.

Putting this process into place wasn't easy at first. Growing up with very little had not only made me a "minimalistic" thinker in terms of what was possible for me, but it had also given me a false sense of virtue around never asking for more. In a way, I felt like dreaming about bigger things for my life was the same as being ungrateful. I feared that people would accuse me of selfishness if I admitted my desire for things like traveling the world, owning a beautiful home, or being a millionaire one day.

This highlights the importance of gratitude, which we'll talk about even more in this chapter and those to come. It brings a beautiful lens to a person's life, allowing them to enjoy each day. But there's a difference between appreciating what you have and feeling bad about daring to hope for more.

I know how difficult dreaming can be. To be honest, I struggled with it myself until about five years ago. In particular, I was so afraid of having my family and friends judge me for my financial goals that I actually sabotaged myself on the way to achieving them. I would give away my money without paying attention because I felt like a bad person for having so much. My mindset around this has shifted dramatically, however. I know that the more money I have, the more impact I can have on the world. Now I see that it's not having money, but what people choose to do with it that determines whether they are a good or bad person.

WRITE IT OUT

Before the conference, I'd occasionally thought about some of my goals, but I'd never written any of them down. Even though I'd heard about people having dream journals and vision boards, I hadn't thought of these practices as being for people like me. After Matthew emphasized the importance of writing down dreams, however, I threw myself into the practice.

Just as Matthew had promised, the effect was powerful. Even before my written goals began manifesting in my life, I instantly felt them shaping my reality by transforming the way I felt on a day to day basis. I got excited listing out my dreams with no self-editing or self-imposed limits and refining those dreams into concrete goals. By physically writing things down, I found I was a lot more intentional about what I wanted to do each day. I could start living the life I wanted in that moment, rather than waiting for my dream life to start.

When I first began writing down my dreams, I resolved to knock three things off my list each year. It didn't take long to realize that I was capable of a lot more than that! I found that I could embark on three major, complex goals each year, while still having plenty of energy for achieving smaller goals every month. Having it all down on paper made it simple to separate the easy goals from the challenging ones, and to pick and choose among them.

Having those goals written down also infused my work life with more meaning than ever. In particular, having those travel goals printed on paper imprinted them on my brain, fueling my excitement and sharpening my focus for any task that lay between me and my dreams. I wasn't just making sales calls anymore. I was working toward my trip to Spain, and nothing—no long hours, and no amount of rejection—was going to stand in my way.

Enjoying your life isn't something that has to wait until you've reached a certain "level." You can be happy today by simply identifying what you want out of life. By having a clear sense of what you're working toward, you're much more likely to enjoy the day-to-day journey.

CREATE VS. COLLECT

Some people genuinely aren't aware that it's possible for them to have more. I find this over and over again when I coach people who feel stuck in a certain habit, a certain way of life, a certain position in the world. They collect whatever life hands them—a job, a relationship, an identity—and do their best to be happy with it. Because they've never been encouraged to think bigger, they never imagine that a different life could be possible for them.

It makes me so happy to help these people realize that they can create a new life for themselves—one that is based on their deepest desires and dreams. I show them how the people who live their best lives are those who work hard to *create* lives they love. Rather than collecting whatever comes their way, these individuals take time to identify what they truly want to include in their lives and what it would take to get it. Their lives are action-based because they fundamentally believe they can have whatever they want.

GRATITUDE—THE POWER BEHIND "POSITIVE VIBES"

The first step in creating a life you love is to cultivate the beautiful, creative energy that comes from a place of appreciation, love, and gratitude.

Once you live with that kind of energy, you can sit down and identify what you'd be excited to accomplish in your life and what you want to be known for. Your most meaningful life might be having a family and raising healthy children, starting and running multiple businesses, helping the environment, or finding a cure for cancer. Everyone's brain is wired in a different way, just like everyone is born with different resources and different strengths. That's why it's imperative to focus on what fulfills *you*. Don't think in terms of how much you can have, but in terms of how much you can do. Picture the life you love and then live in a way that will create that life for yourself. Take action and design a plan to help you achieve your dreams.

TOVAR'S STORY

Tovar left his home in South America and immigrated to the U.S. when he was only fifteen. Because his parents had been unable to accompany him, he was beset by feelings of abandonment, depression, and a lack of belonging. He got it into his head that people didn't want to be around him and that he didn't deserve to be loved. This made him painfully shy. Once, he told me he got nervous just making a phone call to order a pizza. He felt like he wasn't enough and that he lacked the ability to accomplish any of the ideas he had.

When I first started coaching Tovar, we focused on resilience. I listened as he told me about the tough times he had lived through and reminded him that he had no control over those times. Furthermore, I told him, if he remained angry, depressed, or resentful of what had happened to him, anything he tried to create would reflect that negative energy. Whatever was going on inside was going to show on the outside. I reminded Tovar he couldn't change the past, and he couldn't control the future. All he could control was how he responded to challenges when he came up against them and find ways to grow from the challenges he'd faced in the past.

I understand that when people have suffered unfortunate or traumatic experiences, it's easy to lose sight of the importance of gratitude. This was certainly the case for Tovar. But even with all the adversity he had faced and difficulties he'd endured, the reality was, Tovar had managed to make it to the U.S., the land of opportunity. When he and I sat down, and I asked him what he was most grateful for, the more things we listed, the better Tovar's mental and emotional state became. This freed him up to think creatively about the life he wanted.

Tovar and I came up with a vision for his life, writing down his specific dreams for every area. Then we translated those dreams into goals, which gave him a sense of purpose and hope for his day-to-day life. Whether he was cold-calling leads, making phone calls to clients, or doing a presentation, it was all fueled by his vision of starting his own business, buying a house for his family, and creating financial independence. All this gave him an extra level of energy and excitement. It even helped him move easily past rejection. He saw that success in sales was simply a numbers game—a "no" from one lead simply narrows down the search for the "yes," and all he needed was a certain number of yeses to achieve his goal. The more he put the dreaming process into action, the more he realized that he had the power to create anything he wanted in his life.

Throughout our coaching, I watched Tovar evolve from having no self-confidence to having loads of it, and as he put it and the tools I'd shared with him to work in his life, his belief in himself grew. Since our coaching ended, it's been a treat to keep in touch with him and hear how he's continued to transform himself and his life. Today, Tovar runs a web design and digital marketing agency, which offers him plenty of personal freedom. He has long since crossed off some major goals, including taking a scuba diving trip in an underwater cave and finding a place of personal comfort in the midst of uncertainty. To this day, Tovar still keeps a dream journal, making it his aim to cross out three to five goals per year. He likes having a tool that helps him measure what he's already done and watch his life's progress in real time. All in all, Tovar now feels very good about where he is and where he's going. He's realized that he can solve any problem he wants. All he needs to do is make a plan and work hard to achieve his goals.

Deciding what you actually want is a game-changer in creating a life you love. Doing this means you've thought beyond just getting by and surviving. You've thought about what would excite you. You're thriving because you've created future visions you can work toward.

Design Exercise

Using the twelve categories listed above—
physical, emotional, intellectual, spiritual,
psychological, material, adventure, professional,
financial, creative, legacy, character—start
creating your own Dreams List. I challenge you to
go beyond 100—if you're super specific and have
fun with it, it's a lot easier than you might think!

1. _____	21. _____
2. _____	22. _____
3. _____	23. _____
4. _____	24. _____
5. _____	25. _____
6. _____	26. _____
7. _____	27. _____
8. _____	28. _____
9. _____	29. _____
10. _____	30. _____
11. _____	31. _____
12. _____	32. _____
13. _____	33. _____
14. _____	34. _____
15. _____	35. _____
16. _____	36. _____
17. _____	37. _____
18. _____	38. _____
19. _____	39. _____
20. _____	40. _____

41. _____ 71. _____
42. _____ 72. _____
43. _____ 73. _____
44. _____ 74. _____
45. _____ 75. _____
46. _____ 76. _____
47. _____ 77. _____
48. _____ 78. _____
49. _____ 79. _____
50. _____ 80. _____
51. _____ 81. _____
52. _____ 82. _____
53. _____ 83. _____
54. _____ 84. _____
55. _____ 85. _____
56. _____ 86. _____
57. _____ 87. _____
58. _____ 88. _____
59. _____ 89. _____
60. _____ 90. _____
61. _____ 91. _____
62. _____ 92. _____
63. _____ 93. _____
64. _____ 94. _____
65. _____ 95. _____
66. _____ 96. _____
67. _____ 97. _____
68. _____ 98. _____
69. _____ 99. _____
70. _____ 100._____

CHAPTER 3

Why Do You Want It?

When the why gets stronger, the how gets easier.

JIM ROHN

Let's go back to Tyler, the young salesman from chapter 1. While he was able to emerge from his difficult background and transform his life in an inspiring turnaround, there's even more to learn from his story.

Tyler had always known exactly why he was committing to working hard. At first, it had been all about what he *didn't* want—to be a statistic, to end up in jail, to prove all his naysayers right. But as his life progressed, he began identifying all the things he *did* want in his life. He dreamed up a future where he had a beautiful home, an incredible wife, a loving family. Eventually, he wanted to work for himself—to have a thriving business that was his own. He also wanted financial freedom that would allow him to take breaks from working and enjoy amazing experiences without having to worry about money. As his vision expanded, his excitement grew alongside it, to the point that he was put in charge of running his own office after just one year with Vector.

But then, I started noticing a change in Tyler. He would show up for work late, looking run down and like he hadn't got enough sleep. Sometimes, he would have a negative, frustrated energy about him and seem less like the usual happy-go-lucky spirit that filled the whole office with infectious positivity.

In a small workplace, it didn't take long for me to hear what the problem was. Tyler was going out partying. He was spending more time hanging with his old friends than with the positive people he'd met through the company, and the old friends' influence was beginning to creep back into his life.

One day, I sat down with Tyler and asked him, point blank, whether his goals had changed. He blinked, not understanding. "You said you didn't want to be a statistic," I reminded him. "You said you wanted to prove your family wrong about you. But maybe that's changed. Are you fine with wasting your life? Are you good with amounting to nothing, just like your dad said?" I know those words sound pretty harsh. But Tyler and I had always been direct with each other during our coaching sessions. At this pivotal moment in his life, it wasn't the time to beat around the bush.

It's important to have people in your life who aren't afraid to have tough conversations with you. It feels nice when people are always nice, encouraging, or loving, but it won't always get you where you need to be. We all need a little reminder sometimes from the people who know where we're trying to go and aren't willing to let us abandon our dreams.

My blunt reality-check approach made Tyler realize the bigger implications of the choices he'd been making. It brought him back to dreams and goals he had for his life. Did he really want that beautiful family and to provide a beautiful home for them? Did he really want to build a life of financial security and freedom? Asking himself these questions forced Tyler to remember how much progress he had made toward those goals already and how much he'd regret it if he got off track.

I was also candid about reminding Tyler of the potential he had. He'd done the hardest part: identifying what he wanted. He'd made incredible progress in only a year. The things that seemed fun right now—sleeping in, illegal substances, staying out late to party—were just ways to waste the incredible opportunity he'd created for himself.

Tyler knew what he wanted, and he knew what he needed to do in order to get where he wanted to go. He just needed to strengthen his connection with why these action steps were worth taking. He knew he didn't want a life that involved being constantly hungover, running every time he saw a cop car, and ending up on the street. He also knew how good it felt to build a life he loved by using his potential. All he needed was a reminder of all that he'd worked hard to get away from, and all that he was working toward.

Tyler left our conversation with a renewed sense of motivation. He even came up with new ideas for taking action on his goals. Instead of staying up late after work, he planned to get up early so he could take a run while setting his intention for the day. Instead of "relaxing" by partying all night, he decided to find an addictive audiobook or podcast that would push him toward the great things he wanted for his life. It was so satisfying to see Tyler recommit to his dreams by creating a plan to feed his mind. He learned firsthand that even when he got off track in pursuit of his goals, he could use the skills he gained with setting goals, emotional and mental mastery, and resilience to quickly get back on track to the life he always dreamed of.

"WHY" GUIDES YOU

You know how frustrating it is when you're driving in an

unfamiliar area, and suddenly your GPS goes out. You might start taking random turns, following other vehicles, or just pull over out of panic and anxiety. The same thing happens when you somehow lose direction in your life. It can make you frustrated, anxious, angry, depressed, confused, or all of the above.

Sometimes this happens for reasons we can't control. But in my experience, getting off track is usually the result of forgetting the meaning behind what you're doing. Without remembering the "why" behind the actions you take each day, it's very easy to slack off. You can be tempted by distractions from your old way of life. You can fall victim to the negative thoughts programmed by your past experiences. You can lose sight of how strong you are and how far you've already come.

As important as it is to be specific about your goals and dreams, you also need to be specific about the reasons why you identified those goals in the first place. Every day, at least once a day, you have to take a moment to remind yourself where you're trying to get to, and why it's important to get there. You won't get anything accomplished if there isn't a reason pushing you to accomplish it.

SAME JOB, DIFFERENT MEANING

Remember the leadership conference from chapter 2,

the one that helped me dream bigger than I ever had before? Believe it or not, just a year after that conference, I completely lost focus in my work. On paper, I was still performing great, but I had lost all sight of why I was doing what I was doing. The record-breaking sales numbers and number-one corporate rankings suddenly felt meaningless. The big picture—the reason "why"—had disappeared, leaving me empty.

Don't get me wrong, I recognized all the great things that were happening for me, and I knew that I should feel grateful. There were plenty of people who would have loved to be in my shoes, but the achievement and recognition weren't enough for me anymore. My competitive spirit had distracted me from focusing on what was really meaningful to me. I'd been so focused on driving sales numbers and hitting goals that I wasn't connecting with people individually anymore.

The life I loved was about helping people transform their lives by discovering their potential. I didn't just want to break sales records and hit quotas; I wanted to help people create a life they loved. But by that point, I'd totally lost sight of all that. If someone had asked me who my top salespeople were, I wouldn't have had a clue. I started to wonder if I was in the wrong career and if all my time at Vector had been for nothing.

In August of that year, my best friend invited me to a leadership conference with the theme "lead where you are." This conference offered the reality check I needed. I realized that my life felt most meaningful when I was able to impact, influence, and invest in people. When I arrived home, I read over my Dreams List and considered whether the job I currently had matched the life I wanted to live. Ultimately, the answer was yes. I didn't have to quit my job—I just needed to keep my "why" at the forefront of my mind in everything I did.

To do that, I'd have to redefine certain parts of my work life. For example, an obsessive focus on quotas didn't match my dream life. Yes, I would always need to hit certain quotas in order to perform my job well. But rather than focusing on the numbers themselves, I could reframe hitting my quotas as helping my salespeople achieve their dreams of buying homes or getting out of debt. The way I saw it, the more individuals I helped achieve goals that were meaningful to them, the more records we would break and the more goals we would hit.

In re-examining my Dreams List, I was also reminded of a big reason why I'd chosen this career. My family had struggled over the years with a near-constant lack of money. I wanted to be in a position of abundance where I could not only support myself, but also help my family when they needed it. Another important dream of mine was to have a happy, healthy marriage, something I felt was difficult to maintain when finances were bad. My job gave me a unique opportunity to fulfill both these dreams by creating financial freedom for myself. I'd be a fool to throw that away.

The new sense of meaning made all the difference. I aligned my dreams and goals about who I wanted to be and what I wanted to accomplish with the things I was doing. I was still doing the same tasks each day, but the focus on my "why" made them feel more exciting than ever.

THE THREE BRICKLAYERS

When working toward any big goal, you're going to face obstacles. Something will always get in your way. I look at obstacles as tests of whether you actually deserve your dreams or not. Think about it: if accomplishing big dreams was easy, everyone would be doing it. The whole point is that it isn't easy. There will always be obstacles to overcome. Anyone who has ever accomplished something big has had to overcome adversity.

From the outside, we seldom see the adversity in a high achiever's life. Next time you feel jealous when you see someone succeed, stop and consider what that person might have had to overcome to achieve success. (Better yet, just ask them!)

In challenging times, your strong *why* is the only thing that can pull you forward. Meaning gives you a mission, transforming everyday tasks into something inspiring. If you feel dissatisfied in your job the way I did, take a look at your Dreams List and ask yourself: Can you still accomplish those dreams in your line of work? For most people, the answer is yes. All it takes is infusing your daily tasks with a "why" that is truly meaningful to you.

My mentor and friend John Berghoff, CEO of the Flourishing Leadership Institute, loves to tell a story about three bricklayers working together on a project. I'll give you my *CliffsNotes* version of the story. A stranger comes up and asks the first bricklayer what he's doing. "I'm laying bricks," he says. The stranger asks the second bricklayer the same question, and he says, "I'm building a wall." Then the stranger goes to the third bricklayer and asks what he's doing. He answers, "I'm helping build a beautiful place of worship where people can connect with their creator."

All three of these people are doing the same job, but which would you say is doing the most meaningful work? Which bricklayer do you think wakes up and hits the snooze button, versus jumping out of bed and showing up early to get started? Which one do you think goes home feeling better, prouder, and more inspired at the end of the day?

The third bricklayer sees himself as a critical player in an important mission. His bigger "why" makes his daily life so much more exciting and fulfilling.

IDENTIFY YOUR "WHY"

Steve Jobs once said, "If you're working on something exciting that you really care about, you don't have to be pushed. The vision pulls you." If you have a hard time feeling excited or even motivated to do the work in front of you, stop and consider your why. Don't just think how your family, friends, or society would define your role. What does your job mean for you?

When you attach more meaning to the work you're doing, the mundane tasks it involves become part of a bigger picture. When this happens, you don't feel like you're forced to do something. Instead, you're drawn to it. You've been given an amazing opportunity to create something great. Don't waste this opportunity.

Design Exercise

At the end of your life, what are some things that would make it feel as though you fully used the days you were given?

PART TWO

Your Master Plan

Vision without action is merely a dream. Action without vision just passes the time. Vision with action can change the world.

JOEL A. BARKER

CHAPTER 4

Identify Your Non-Negotiables

Once you make a decision, the universe conspires to make it happen.

RALPH WALDO EMERSON

The last chapter ended with a story about how I lost motivation and focus for my work, only to recover it in a big way through reconnecting to my "why." I'd love to tell you that from that moment forward, everything was smooth sailing, moving from one high point to the next. But as you probably know, life doesn't usually work like that.

Yes, I enjoyed an amazing renewal in my passion and sense of purpose for my work. But by the end of that year, I was trying to get so much done that I was constantly low on energy. While my work life was excelling, everything else in my life was starting to redline. I was feeling physically and mentally run down. I felt like I was constantly under the gun, running late, forgetting things. And despite making good money, I still seemed to have a hard time balancing my finances.

Lucky for me, I had just started working with a great leadership coach named Trent Booth. I called him up and confessed how I was struggling. I wanted to drive the business' growth and be there for my people, but I also wanted to take care of myself. It just seemed impossible to get everything done.

I'll never forget Trent's response: "Okay, but what are you *actually* going to get done?"

At first, I was confused by his question. I started repeating all the things I'd just told him were on my plate. But he stopped me.

"There's a difference," Trent said, "between wanting to do things and actually committing to the actions to execute them. You can want to do things all day, but you're not going to do anything unless it becomes a "need to.""

MAKE IT A NEED

To explain, Trent asked about the things that needed to

get done. If an email needed to be sent, if a bill needed to be paid, if an employee needed extra coaching, did I find a way to make it happen?

Yes, I said, absolutely. Everything that *needed* to get done always got done.

Trent then pointed out that things I didn't consider needs always got pushed aside—things such as getting enough sleep, working out on a regular basis, preparing healthy meals. It seemed so obvious when he pointed it out. No matter how much I said I wanted those things, they never actually happened.

Trent added that many of the things I'd listed as wants were, in fact, deserving of need-status because they played a vital role to ensuring I delivered on the higher-level needs. For example, I really needed to eat right and work out in order to maintain the energy it took to serve my people at the highest level. Trent also pointed out that not every need was as complicated or time-intensive as I thought it was. For example, in my mind, I had equated eating right with planning and preparing all my own meals. When I didn't have time to do meal prep, I ended up going to work with no food, which led to last-minute visits to the drive-through. But as I thought about it, I realized that while it would be nice to have time every week for meal prep, it wasn't the only way to provide good fuel for my body. What I *needed* was to eat healthy—that could happen by simply picking up a smoothie or salad from an organic café or grocery store. I could also space out the meal prep sessions to be every month, instead of every week.

As for working out, my busy schedule at work seemed to make it impossible to hit the gym. I felt bad about taking any time out of my workday, because I wanted to serve my people as much as possible. However, I couldn't deny that I did my best work when I was feeling my best physically. Operating on fumes made me irritable, anxious, and short-tempered with my staff. While it would be nice to have unlimited availability for my staff, I realized that I had to spend time investing in myself in order to be the best leader I could be.

This, too, turned out to be a lot easier than I expected. I sat down with my staff and explained that, moving forward, there would be times when they wouldn't be able to reach me because I needed to take time to refuel my energy by working out. "If I don't do this," I said, "I won't be the best coach and leader I can be for you." To my surprise, they were all unanimously supportive. "Then go!" they said. It turned out that they had noticed my low energy and short fuse for quite a while, and they were more than happy to let me pursue a solution.

It was just a matter of days before I began seeing the difference. After spending an hour in yoga class or the boxing ring, I was in a great mood the rest of the day, able to have fun and serve my staff at the highest level.

The conversation with Trent made a massive impact on me. Before that, I felt like I never had any time for myself because of all the other things people expected of me. I realized that the only way I'd be able to serve and lead at the highest level was by identifying and honoring my personal needs first. There would always be a lot of things that sounded fun, appealing, or helpful. But until I saw something as a non-negotiable—a necessary step in accomplishing my dreams—I'd never commit to getting it done.

IDENTIFY WHAT FUELS YOU

When I saw how well my staff responded to my commitment around working out, I began thinking about how this idea of non-negotiables could help all of us improve our performance, not to mention our lives as a whole. We started talking as a group about the things that refueled us mentally, emotionally, physically, or spiritually—the things that helped us perform at our highest level. Some of my team members said they needed a real lunch break. No more wolfing down meals between sales calls, they said. One said he wanted to take a twenty-minute nap during the day.

Others on my staff were fueled more by emotional factors. One guy said that he was fueled by getting at least one quality night out with his girlfriend every week. Another guy said that his fuel came from spending time with his little brothers and sisters, taking them to the park and strengthening their family bond. For one person, refueling came in a spiritual form—he needed to pray and read the Bible each day in order to feel like he was bringing his best self. A few said that all it took for them to do their best was a few words of affirmation from me.

This discussion showed how each of us had a very individual set of needs for operating at our highest levels. When we let these needs slip into the "want" category, our performance and happiness started to slip. But when we made time for these things, each of us had a much higher level of energy and were able to bring our best to the office.

Pause + Reflect

Take a moment to identify some of the things that refuel your energy. What is it that gets you feeling invincible?

HONOR YOUR NEEDS

As fun as it was to explore the things that fueled our tank, I knew from my own experience that making these needs into non-negotiables would require some boundary setting, both individually and cooperatively. I told my team that I needed their accountability to ensure that I honored my non-negotiables, and without hesitation, they began kicking me out of the office at seven p.m. so that I could get to the gym for an hour. They even agreed to stop bringing french fries into the office to help me maintain my resolve about eating healthy food. (And I love french fries!)

My team members were incredible about honoring my needs, so I made sure to honor theirs in return. For the staff member who said he needed a nap to be his best self, I popped into his office each day to tell him when would be a good time for him to close his door and get twenty minutes of sleep. Wouldn't you know, it totally worked. After twenty minutes, he'd open his door again, looking energized and ready to rock and roll. For those who said they needed encouragement, all I had to do was take them aside and tell them something they'd done well that day, and they'd be glowing with motivation for the rest of it.

Such an exercise can be used in a family environment. One of my assistants, Rebecca, uses it with her family. She asks them what makes them happy and what they need to feel like an important part of the family. This can help involve kids in certain decision-making processes. They may express that they want to create or help with something specific, even chores. Kids are likely to take more ownership of tasks when these are their ideas.

A lot of people go through life without asking themselves what their non-negotiables are. They wake up and go, go, go. They work themselves to death fulfilling all the expectations that others have of them while never making time to address *their* needs. Sometimes, it's just out of habit; other times, it's because they feel selfish asking for what they need. They react to things that come their way, and don't take time to first ask themselves what they want for the day and then act accordingly. But by not being intentional about the things they do or the decisions they make, little by little, people can lose their sense of passion, purpose, and fulfillment in life.

I've known so many people-pleasers who constantly sacrificed their own needs in order to fulfill the needs of others. While their intentions were good, they didn't realize that they really weren't helping others as much as they thought. In some cases, they were actually hurting the people they were trying to help. If you constantly make yourself available to anyone around you, you're enabling those people to constantly lean on you and never learn to help themselves. What happens when you finally run out of resources to help them?

If you truly want to help someone else become their best, you have to start by setting yourself up to be your best. It's not selfish to prioritize your own needs. When you're at your best, you're going to serve the people around you at your highest level. Think of it this way: you can't pour someone a full glass of water from an empty jug. If you're only 50 percent full, you can't give 70 percent to your family, friends, or workplace. The only way to serve at your highest level is from a place of overflow.

"NICE TO'S" VS. "MUST DO'S"

If you're like me, your Dreams List can get really long,

really fast. It's not unusual for me to have upward of 100 goals on my list at one time! So how do you decide which of these are non-negotiables?

The key is dividing your list of goals into two lists—the "nice to's" and the "must do's." Go through each goal and ask yourself: If you weren't able to accomplish it, would you be fine with this? Those are the "nice-to" goals. Then ask yourself which goals would make your life feel incomplete if you didn't accomplish them. Those are your "must do's," the non-negotiables that demand your commitment and priority.

Don't stress out in dividing up your goals this way. These lists aren't set in stone. Once you've listed the steps it would take to accomplish a goal, you might realize that the goal means less or more to you than you originally thought. Remember, just because you aren't committed to taking action on a goal today, that doesn't mean you have to delete it from your Dreams List. Over the years, as we grow, our priorities change. Things that were once important to us don't seem as important anymore, and other things that were just "nice to's" become a lot more important. You may pass over certain goals today, only to come back to them later in life.

Turning something from a "nice to" into a "must do" is a big mental shift. You need to analyze your situation to decide what you're actually committed to working toward. Take time not only to consider your goals, but also to break down what it will take to achieve them. Once you break down your goals into step-by-step components, it'll be easier to decide just how committed to them you are.

This starts with smart decision-making. Whenever you go to do something, ask yourself, why does this matter? How will it help you accomplish the things that are important to you? If you can't find a reason why that thing matters, then it probably won't get done...and that's fine! For the things that do matter, it's not hard to include that crucial *why* component.

After you decide whether or not a task matters, ask yourself what it will take for you to get it done. Do you need to work out five mornings a week for twenty minutes, or three evenings per week for an hour? Do you need to get up an hour early so that you can make yourself a great cup of coffee and spend some time reading? Maybe your "must do" is just a once-a-month requirement, like my meal prep sessions. It all depends on the goal itself and how it serves you best.

Once you've outlined the action steps your "must do" requires, you're in a better position to think about commitment. Can you picture yourself doing what it takes to accomplish that goal? Can you prioritize your time and effort around it? As Trent reminded me on that life-giving coaching call, it's always okay to not be committed to something, as long as you're honest with yourself about it. In fact, it's much better to throw out the "nice to's" than to stress out about something that you're not truly willing to devote your effort and resources to.

On the other hand, if something is truly a "must do" for you, be real with yourself about that. Give yourself a strong enough reason *why* you want to do something. Then, take the right steps and commit to getting it done.

GET OTHERS INVOLVED

As soon as you identify your non-negotiables, you gain a sense of direction. And as soon as you involve the people who care about you, you'll be amazed at how quickly you make progress in that direction. As we discussed in the last chapter, a supportive community is tremendously helpful in keeping you on track with your goals.

Imagine you've been planning a trip to Mexico. Once you've decided that the trip is a "must do," you commit to saving at least $100 per week. You cut down on your mindless spending, request the time off work, and start sharing your plans with friends. Not only do they get excited for you, but they also start to help you make progress toward your goal. If they see you spending too much at happy hour or considering a new pair of expensive shoes, they can easily keep you in check and ask, "Do you prefer extra drinks, or your dream trip to Mexico?"

Don't worry that commitment to your goals will make you seem rigid or "not fun." For the people who truly care about you, it will be a joy to hold you accountable and see you succeed. You'll be amazed by how ready people are to support you in reaching your non-negotiables.

Pause + Reflect

What is something you have been wanting to do, but it seems to always get pushed to the side? What would it take to make it a "must do" instead of a "nice to?"

IDENTIFY GOALS, SET TIMELINES, TAKE ACTION

Once you've identified your non-negotiable goals, you can make actual plans for execution. First of all, consider the timeline that makes sense for each specific goal. Is this a goal you want to accomplish in the next five or ten years, or is it more of a lifetime goal? Knowing the timeline will not only help you make progress, but also help you make smarter decisions about how you spend your time and resources.

EXAMPLE #1: BUYING A HOUSE IN PUERTO RICO

I dream all the time of having a vacation house in the Arizona desert, a cabin in the mountains, and a bungalow on the beach in California. But I am one hundred percent positive that I must own a home in Puerto Rico. It all comes down to my "why." I want that Puerto Rico house so that my family will always have a place to come together. I picture hosting family reunions there, offering hospitality to extended family and friends, spending six months there working remotely while enjoying a slower pace of life. I've determined to buy or build out the land for our Puerto Rico home in the next five years, and I've set up a series of action steps to get me there.

While the mountain cabin or the desert home might be easier to accomplish, I'm not prioritizing it, because it doesn't hold the same meaning for me. Even if somebody showed up with a gorgeous cabin at a great price, I probably wouldn't buy it, because I'm focused on accomplishing my "must dos" for the next five years.

EXAMPLE #2: BRINGING THE SPARK BACK TO A RELATIONSHIP

The same process applies to a non-material goal. I had a client come to me with the goal of improving her sixteen-year marriage. She and her husband really loved each other, but during the past several years, she'd found herself envying other couples' seeming closeness. She didn't know when her marriage had stopped being like that—all business and no fun—but she wanted it to change. She wanted to be able to plan adventures and have fun again, but it was hard to know how to start. It seemed like she and her husband were never on the same page anymore.

The first question I asked is whether she thought it would be nice for her marriage to improve, or did she *need* it to improve? There was no right or wrong answer, I told her. For some people, having a pretty good marriage where you get along, raise a family, and don't hate each other is enough to feel satisfied. But for others, they can't bear the idea of getting to the end of their life and feeling like they missed out on being madly in love.

This client said her marriage was extremely important to her. With that established, we jumped into making a detailed plan. After all, even though changing a relationship is a lot more involved than buying a house, it's still a concrete goal and requires action steps to get there.

We researched books she could read to make sure she was showing up in her relationship at her best. We brainstormed activities that her husband liked and discussed how she could organize date nights around them. We talked about how she could be honest with her husband about how important their relationship was to her without being negative or overwhelming. We talked about different elements that had helped others improve their relationships—seminars, conferences, counseling—and how to incorporate these things in a positive way. I advised her to start by suggesting a couples' retreat at a destination they would both enjoy. It would offer them an escape from regular life, an opportunity to let go of their obligations, and have the types of exciting experiences they'd had when they first started dating. Through a series of intentional actions, they were able to reignite the excitement and fun in their relationship!

EXAMPLE #3: THE "STUFF" VERSUS THE EXPERIENCE

As humans, we're prone to overanalyzing the things that are most important to us and overcomplicating the process of achieving them. The truth is that most goals aren't that hard to accomplish when you have a strong "why" behind them. It's the vague goals—the ones empty of personal meaning—that are hardest to take action on.

When I was in my early twenties, I was determined to be

part of a country club. The status of having that membership was something important to me. It was proof of having achieved something, of being identified as a successful person.

Twelve years later, though, I looked at that goal on my Dreams List and took it off. From where I am in my life now, I can see how ego-driven that goal was at that specific time of my life. It didn't hold deep personal meaning for me. I could happily reach the end of my life and never think twice about missing out on the "status" a country club confers.

However, there are two things a country club in my area offers that are meaningful to me: great brunch and access to boats. So while I threw out the country club membership goal, I wrote down two new goals. The first was weekly brunch dates with my husband. The second was joining our local boat club. For now, I feel great about renting a boat once a quarter. That way, I could take my family and friends out for a day on the water without having to worry about maintenance, insurance, and all the other headaches involved in being a boat owner.

See why it's so important to analyze your Dreams List every year? It's a vital chance to remind yourself why certain goals are important to you and assess which ones are no longer in alignment with your vision for your best life. It also helps you stay on track with the goals that are harder to accomplish. When Tyler got off track from his goals, the thing that got him back was remembering why he'd set those goals in the first place. To avoid getting overwhelmed by doubt and difficulty, keep focusing on your non-negotiable goals, and keep asking yourself *why*.

Design Exercise

Identify the top 20 non-negotiables on your Dreams List. Make sure to write down why they're non-negotiable.

1. Goal:_____

   Why: _____

2. Goal:_____

   Why: _____

3. Goal:_____

   Why: _____

4. Goal:_____

   Why: _____

5. Goal:_____

   Why: _____

6. Goal:_____

   Why: _____

7. Goal:_____

   Why: _____

8. Goal:_____

   Why: _____

9. Goal:_____

   Why: _____

10. Goal: _____

    Why: _____

11. Goal: _____

    Why: _____

12. Goal: _____

    Why: _____

13. Goal: _____

    Why: _____

14. Goal: _____

    Why: _____

15. Goal: _____

    Why: _____

16. Goal: _____

    Why: _____

17. Goal: _____

    Why: _____

18. Goal: _____

    Why: _____

19. Goal: _____

    Why: _____

20. Goal: _____

    Why: _____

CHAPTER 5

Create Timeframes

If you talk about it, it's a dream...if you schedule it, it's real.

TONY ROBBINS

Shortly after I moved to Texas, I started hearing about a couple called Mr. and Mrs. White. The office manager raved about how incredible these people were, and what an amazing story they had.

By the time I met the Whites, I was convinced that I would love them, and I wasn't wrong. They were not only sweet people, but also incredibly humble, even in light of their tremendous accomplishments: a happy marriage, a gorgeous home, a string of successful businesses. From the outside, it looked as though the Whites had followed an uncomplicated path to success. But I knew that their story went a lot deeper, and one day, I had the chance to sit down with them and hear how they created a dream life for themselves out of nothing.

Marcus White grew up in difficult circumstances. He dropped out of high school to help his family pay the bills and had no formal education beyond his GED. At the time he met his wife Jenny, he had no money and no prospects; he lived in a tiny apartment with only a mattress to sleep on.

Nevertheless, Marcus had a vision for his life. He wanted to do more than just get by—he wanted to create something. Shortly after marrying Jenny, he got a job selling waterbeds. That job, he said, transformed his life. His fellow salespeople were very focused on personal growth and development, and they exposed him to the power of positive thinking. While Marcus wasn't a natural salesman, the company trained him in the process of setting goals, writing them down, and using his job to move his life forward. It was there he was given a tape titled "The Power of the Inner Winner" that would forever change his life. (We'll talk more about this later, in chapter 9.)

Along with listening to tapes on personal growth and development, Marcus started every morning by looking at his goals and committing them to memory, so that his subconscious would keep him on track. He made it his mantra to ask, in each moment of decision, whether what he was doing would get him closer to his goal or further away from it. He started by setting one-year goals and quickly moved on to setting five-year goals. Because of his discipline and commitment, he soon found himself achieving those five-year goals in half the time he'd expected to. That's when he realized it was time to think bigger.

One of Marcus' early goals was to have a car that didn't break down. This sounds pretty simple, but it wasn't easy for a young couple with two kids who were just starting to pull themselves out of their financial straits. One day, Marcus saw an ad for Landmark Chevrolet and decided to go in for an interview. The head salesman asked him, "What makes you think you can sell cars?" Marcus responded, "I don't see why not." Within six months, Marcus was working in the finance department and earning $45,000 a year. He also got a great interest rate on a brand-new car.

Having seen the power of goal-setting, Marcus set a new goal for himself: to be financially independent in five years. Granted, he had no idea how that would happen. All he had was a GED and scattered work experience in grocery stores, a mattress shop, and now a car dealership. On paper, he didn't have the qualifications to get the kind of job that would guarantee financial independence.

Even without those qualifications, though, Marcus was

making a lot of money for the time. At one point, he bought a boat, only to find it was too tall to fit in his garage. He did some looking around and realized there were no places to store boats in his area. Guess what happened next? Marcus made it his goal to start a boat storage business that would bring the financial independence he desired. Again, he had no idea how it would happen, but he wrote it down and set his subconscious to working on it.

It wasn't long before Marcus crossed paths with a local man looking to sell a chunk of land. He was asking $100,000; Marcus showed up to their meeting with a cashier's check made out for $50,000—all he had in savings. The man turned Marcus' offer down, so Marcus took the check off the table, put it back in his briefcase, and got up to walk out. "Wait!" the man shouted. A few minutes later, Marcus was a landowner.

The business Marcus started, Woodland Boat and RV Storage, became the catalyst for all the couple's other businesses and ventures. Today, Marcus and Jenny run a business park, a RV shop, retail shops, and rental properties. It's safe to say that Marcus and Jenny are a power couple. They're living an incredible life in which they can do everything they want to do without having to worry about money.

Marcus attributes most of this success to the power of

writing down goals. It didn't matter if life took them three steps forward and two steps backward; with his goals written down on a piece of paper, he says, his brain had a roadmap of where to go.

I couldn't agree more. Ever since I created my first Dreams List in 2006, I've learned in every area of my life that writing down goals makes all the difference. Adding timeframes to these goals kicks them into high gear.

HELP YOURSELF ACHIEVE

We've talked about the importance of specificity with your goals. Timeframe is a particularly crucial way to get specific. Setting a timeframe for your goal creates a sense of urgency. Humans are natural procrastinators; consciously or subconsciously, we tend to put things off whenever we can. But when you see a timeframe written down, it registers in your brain as being extra important. Better yet, it programs your brain to automatically respond. Like Marcus White with the five-year financial independence goal, you naturally begin to make decisions that help you fulfill your goals within the timeframe you've set for yourself. Timeframes also make goal-setting incredibly practical. If you set a one-year goal for yourself, you can easily break it down into smaller targets for each quarter, month, week, and day.

My brother Josh always dreamed of being a firefighter.

When he was young, he had a hard time sticking with school. He hated staying home to study while his friends were out having fun. He felt like he was missing out on all the good things his social life had to offer.

I saw this frustration and tried to help Josh see the greater good that he was pursuing. I told him that small sacrifices he was making now were going to create an incredible future for him. If he gave himself at least five years, he would see his hard work pay off, and eventually he would set himself up forever. I reminded him of his goal: if he wanted to apply for the fire academy, he needed to set a specific timeframe to take on some temporary pain for extraordinary gains down the line.

He created a timeline for himself and made plans on what he would focus on in that time. Less than five years from the time he set his goals and wrote them down, he was graduating from the city of Miami Fire Academy and officially hired to work at his dream station!

Never underestimate the power of the human mind. When you see something written in front of you, you simultaneously hear it in your mind. Together, these two sensory triggers program that idea into your brain. Not only do you retain the information, but your brain immediately starts working on ways to make it happen.

THE POWER OF DEATH

There's nothing like death to remind you of life and the urgency of every moment. After surviving that car accident at age eighteen, I realized for the first time how short life is and became determined to never again waste my days. But as time passed, that determination got a little loose. I still thought about it a lot, but I didn't always hold myself to the same standard of action.

That all changed after my cousin died in 2006. We were the same age—just twenty-three—and his death came as a huge shock. We were so young and doing so much good in the world. Even though I knew from my own near-death experience that life was short, I guess somewhere in the back of my mind, I thought God would make sure we both lived long enough to do all the good we were capable of.

Since the age of nineteen, I'd always worked hard to do good for myself and the world, knowing that every day could be my last. But when my cousin died, I thought for the first time about whether I was making enough of an effort to be the best person I could be. Was I as patient as I wanted to be? Was I as loving as I wanted to be? Where was I stressed, anxious, frustrated, and what did I have to do to ensure these things didn't define my life? Personal growth became just as important a goal as finishing school and finding a job I loved.

When my sister died in 2013, it renewed my sense of urgency all over again to make every day count. I didn't want to be the person who never evaluates their life until they're eighty years old. Even though I'd been systematically accomplishing my dreams for a number of years, I needed to feel sure that I was steering my life toward a legacy I could be proud of. I took a long drive up the coast of Florida, sat on the beach for a day, and rewrote my entire Dreams List from scratch. I came up with over one hundred new dreams in just a few hours.

Since that day, each year, I've set aside time to look at and evaluate my goals based on the legacy I want to leave behind. When my time is up, I want to confidently say that I used all the gifts and resources I was given to create a life I can be proud of.

MAKE TIME TO CELEBRATE

In the past, I cared a lot about how the world saw me. I wanted to be viewed as high-achieving and successful, with the material rewards to show for it. But in the days and weeks of reflection after my sister's death, I started thinking more about how my friends and family saw me. When my time was up, I didn't want them to remember me as a workaholic who was never around. I wanted to be remembered as a passionate and inspiring person who worked hard but always made time to love and care for the people around her.

It felt more important than ever to spend time with my family. Family vacations had always been on my Dreams List, but now they moved from "nice to" to "must do." As a result, instead of having a funeral for my sister, we held a celebration of her life and planned our first family vacation in sixteen years. We took an incredible trip to Napa (it's what she wanted to do for her thirtieth birthday, which she never got to) where we spent hours remembering all the great moments we'd had, and giving thanks for all the love and blessings we enjoyed as a family.

I realized during that trip that I needed to do more celebrating in my own life. I didn't want to get so caught up with what I was trying to build or create for the long-term that I lost track of all the good things happening today. Sometimes if you're overly focused on the future, you risk missing what's happening in the now. My sister's death urged me to not be so focused on the future that I missed the joys of the present.

That family vacation following my sister's death was a wake-up call for our whole family. We all realized that there might not always be a "later," and we committed to gathering as a family at least once a year. Whether it means taking an expensive trip together or just gathering together at my dad's house for a staycation, we've made time every year to celebrate, enjoy, and give thanks for each other.

It's very easy to beat yourself up when you work hard for something that just doesn't happen for you. However, that anger and frustration won't get you any closer to achieving your goals.

In contrast, gratitude and celebration are powerful forces in pushing you forward. Instead of being stressed about what I haven't achieved yet, I want to laugh and celebrate how far I've come and what I've accomplished up to now. Focus and motivation are important in working toward my goals, but to truly live a life I love, it's important to make sure that I'm having fun along the way.

Design Exercise

Take the non-negotiables you listed at the end of the last chapter and give them a deadline/ timeframes. This is the first step in making these dreams come to life. Once you identify what you want to get done this year, it will help you to prioritize what you focus on. By breaking your big goals into smaller steps, you'll find they are not as scary or overwhelming, and get done much faster!

1 Year Goals	**3–5 Year Goals**
Decade Goals	**Lifetime Goals**

CHAPTER 6

Decide Your Action Steps

Some people want it to happen...Some people make it happen.

MICHAEL JORDAN

In May 2002, I was looking for a summer job to help fund a semester abroad in London that fall. By that time in my life, I'd been living on my own for two years and was responsible for my own bills and school tuition. The study abroad program would cost an additional $5,000 on top of my university tuition. And, as luck would have it, I'd just lost one of my two part-time jobs thanks to a coworker forgetting that they'd promised to cover one of my shifts. Frustration kicked in. How was I going to hit my goal? How was I going to have enough money to go to London? What was I going to do?

With all these questions swimming in my head, I drove to school to use the computer lab. That's when, on my way through the parking lot, I looked down and saw the Vector Marketing business card that would change my world forever. "Student work! Meaningful job experience. Resume builder. Scholarships offered! No experience required!" it said, seeming to speak directly to me.

FAST START

At Vector, I moved quickly from the application to the interview process, where I learned that employees had earned as much as $10,000 and even $20,000 in just one summer. That sounded like an incredible opportunity... but could I really pull it off? I wasn't sure. Just making the amount I needed for a semester abroad seemed like a pretty daunting goal.

I sat down with the manager and asked him what it would take for me to make $5,000 over the summer. He countered with a question of his own: How many weeks could I work before I had to leave? I told him that I could be all in for the next ten weeks, right up until the program started in the second week of August.

He pulled out a piece of paper and mapped out the end of May, all of June and July, and the first week of August, breaking down the sales I'd need to make at what average amount per order to get to $5,000 in earnings. Once he did this, the process seemed ridiculously easy. According to my averages, I needed only ten to twelve sales a week, which worked out to about three or four appointments, five or six days a week. After pulling double shifts six days a week at my old restaurant job, that schedule sounded totally doable.

I told the manager that while the opportunity of selling Cutco seemed great, I still needed to hold on to my second job. I needed it to pay my bills, and also save up some spending money for my trip abroad. He heard me out on this and offered to show me what it would take to make $10,000 that summer instead. We broke it down again, and it still seemed doable.

My family and friends thought I was crazy. They never believed that in a single summer, I'd make $10,000 selling knives. Imagine their surprise when I got to the end of those two and a half months with $22,000 to my name. I couldn't believe it!

In my first week, I surpassed my goal of $1,000 and made $1,600. This time was such an eye opener for me. It was the first time I realized I could set a goal, break it down, commit to it, and actually see it happen. It felt so great to exceed my goal that every week that followed, I made it my goal to go beyond my minimum.

Since that summer, my approach to goals has never

changed. I take every "must do" on my Dreams List, identify what it will take to get there, and break it down into small action steps. This strategy has carried over from work into every other part of my life. I've seen over and over that little actions, performed consistently, add up to incredible results.

Just as having big goals makes your daily tasks a lot less tedious, breaking down big goals makes them much less overwhelming. It's so much easier to break things down and commit to small actions than it is to look at the big picture. When small actions add up, they can create big results.

Don't get me wrong, the big picture is necessary to keep in mind. However, to get to the big picture, focus on the small actions.

EXAMPLE #1: SKIP HAPPY HOUR

I recently coached a client named Alex, who worked part-time as a fitness coach. He ran his business out of his car, traveling to clients' homes or different gyms around town with all his training gear in the trunk. He really wanted to have his own workout facility. Without having to spend so much time commuting, he could focus on designing programs that pushed people further. The only problem with this dream was that he had no idea where to start.

Just as my Cutco manager had done with me, I sat down with Alex and asked him what this goal would look like when it became reality. He went through the details of what he wanted to do at his training facility, how big the space would need to be, what kind of equipment, and how many employees he'd need. As we got into the details, I could see that Alex was getting discouraged. The goal felt too big, and he was starting to feel overwhelmed.

I assured Alex that his goal was totally doable. Obviously, he wasn't going to achieve it overnight. But if we broke it down, he could easily knock it out in three years or less.

After putting some numbers to his details, we calculated that Alex would need about $10,000 to make this dream a reality. Then we broke that number down to a monthly amount. We even set options for monthly amounts in a one-year, two-year, and three-year period. Then we broke it down even further. How much would Alex have to save each week to get this done in a year?

The answer turned out to be $192 per week. This number really opened Alex's eyes. It was about the same amount he spent in a weekend going out for drinks with his friends. He realized that if he quit going out for happy hour and instead invited his friends over for drinks at his house, he could save up enough to start his workout facility in a year. Talk about a little pain for a lot of gain.

Alex didn't look back. He fully committed to this plan and ended up saving the $10,000 he needed in just nine months. In less than a year, he'd accomplished something that he previously believed was impossible for him.

EXAMPLE #2: CREATE FLEXIBLE OPTIONS

Another client, Melissa, told me that she deeply wanted to take her family on a vacation to Europe. She'd been dreaming of it for years, had the whole trip planned out in her mind, and had even ensured that she could take the time off from work. I asked what was stopping her, and the answer, unsurprisingly, was money. Flights for her family of five, two weeks of hotels and meals, admission prices for all the activities she wanted them to do…it was just overwhelming.

When we started researching the prices around all those elements, we made some interesting discoveries. For instance, it was cheaper for her to rent a home in each destination than to pay for hotels. That also would help her family cut down on meal costs, since they could buy groceries instead of eating out for every meal. We took a look at flights and found that going before or after the busy season would make a big difference in the costs of the flights. According to our calculations, Melissa could make her dream trip happen for $7,000. If she had to, she could even scale back some of her desired activities and make it happen for $5,000.

With this flexible budget in mind, we broke the trip down by year, month, and week, again with two different time-frame options. If Melissa put aside $100 per paycheck, she and her family could go to Europe that next year. If she put aside $50 per check, they could do it in two years.

Just like Alex, Melissa got incredibly motivated once she saw how easily she could attain her goal. She ended up saving the full $7000 she needed in just six months and going on a mini-vacation in the fall. She had the confidence to know that she could make a plan, figure out what it would take, and go make it happen.

The moral of both stories? You gain confidence when you break big goals down into small, doable steps. Just about anybody can put aside $50 per week by making just a few changes to your lifestyle. Maybe for you it means making your own coffee instead of buying it at Starbucks. Maybe it means wearing what's already in your closet, instead of buying new outfits every month. Maybe it means quitting smoking so that you aren't spending money on cigarettes anymore. (Plus, you'll achieve a bonus goal—feeling better and getting healthier!)

The same incremental approach applies to goals that aren't material—having a better relationship, overcoming depression or anxiety, or learning a cool new skill. Even goals that don't cost money can be broken down into yearly/monthly/weekly/daily action steps that make the big picture much less overwhelming and let you experience easy gains that speed the process along.

Ultimately, every goal comes down to good guidance, willpower, and small, incremental actions that build up over time.

BUILDING BRICK BY BRICK

There's a story I love about the actor Will Smith. Back when he was a kid, his dad taught him and his brother about perseverance and willpower by having them rebuild a wall for his shop.

Once when he was interviewed, I heard him share how this lesson helped him achieve so much in his life. He explained how most people see a daunting task, and it's difficult for them to take the first step when they are just looking at how big the task is. Will said this is what always set him apart. He stated,

> "The task was never huge to me, it was always one brick. You don't set out to build a wall. You don't say 'I'm going to build the biggest, baddest, greatest wall that's ever been built.' You don't start there. You say, 'I'm going to lay this brick as perfectly as a brick can be laid. You do that every single day. And soon, you have a wall."

Do your current goals look overwhelming to you? Do they seem like they'll take forever to accomplish? Or have you broken them down into the simple step of just laying one brick as perfectly as possible? Make things simpler for yourself by identifying the small steps you need to take in order to achieve a bigger goal or vision. Commit to taking those small actions consistently, and you'll accomplish way more than you ever thought possible in less time than you would believe.

Design Exercise

Time to break down your one-year goals from the last chapter's exercise. What actions need to be taken monthly, weekly, and even daily to achieve them? Setting short-term goals with timeframes is the key to staying on track!

Monthly

Weekly

Daily

CHAPTER 7

Schedule a Fire under Your A**

You don't have to be great to get started, but you have to get started to be great.

LES BROWN

When Chris started as my coaching client, he came with plenty of dreams for how he wanted his life to look. He even had plans for how to accomplish some of them. His problem was that he didn't get a lot done. His Dreams List was more like a series of wishes than real goals.

Together, we detailed the specifics of Chris' dreams, put together the action steps he'd need for accomplishing each one, and broke down the yearly/monthly/weekly timeframe around them. But then came the big piece he was missing: I told him that if he truly wanted to make his dreams a reality, he needed to put these action items into his schedule.

Chris had always been a day-to-day kind of person. He went to school, paid his bills, and showed up for his daily responsibilities, but he was essentially living in survival mode. He knew what it would take to really thrive, but he hadn't made it happen, because he didn't have a sense of *when* it needed to happen.

For Chris, scheduling was the step that changed everything. It gave his dreams a new sense of relevance and urgency, taking them out of the "maybe one day" category and making them a part of his daily life. Knowing what he had to get done, and knowing when he had to do it, made it easy for him to hit his monthly, quarterly, and annual goals. Soon enough, the dreams that once seemed far off weren't so far off anymore.

As Chris accomplished each goal, he also expanded his vision of what was possible. He went from simply wanting financial stability to running his own digital marketing company. He went from wanting to travel more to getting certified for scuba diving and taking his dream vacation.

Chris had no idea he could accomplish so much, let alone how quickly he could do it, just by programming it into his schedule. Once he decided, "I'm doing X this year," he identified his action steps, created his timeframe, and scheduled himself toward success.

It's one thing to know the steps you need to take. It's another thing to actually make time for those actions in your daily schedule. Once you move your goals from paper to your calendar, you'll see your dreams become reality.

INTERRUPT YOUR INTERRUPTIONS

Remember the breakdown process we talked about in the last chapter? That process will get you nowhere if you don't plug it into your calendar. If Alex hadn't scheduled "drinks at home with friends" for his Friday night, he would probably have ended up at happy hour again, and it would have taken a lot longer to save the $10,000 he needed to achieve his dream.

Of course, we all know that even the best-planned schedules get interrupted from time to time. Sometimes, those interruptions are so consistent that we subconsciously learn to plan around them. Maybe you really want to start attending a yoga class once a week, but something always comes up to get in your way. You left work late, and now there's too much traffic to get there on time. Your friends are going out and want you to go along. You stayed up late last night, and now all you want to do is fall asleep to some Netflix.

Scheduling your dreams helps you interrupt those interruptions when they happen. When you know that *ping!* in your calendar is an action item attached to your dream, it's a lot easier to make sure interruptions don't take you off track.

You can also break your scheduled action items down into "nice to's" and "must do's," just as you did with your big-picture goals. Your "must do's" are the ones that can't be changed—you have to get them done that day, at that time, or they won't get done at all. The "nice to's" are the ones that can be moved around if needed. If you're at an appointment that runs late, or a family member needs a hand with something, you can move that "nice to" action item to another time.

Be flexible. While it's important to have a plan, it's just as important to be flexible with that plan. On any given day, you might get one or two important things done. There might also be a couple of other things you plan to get done but need to move around. This is where the flexibility portion comes in.

THE YEARLY/QUARTERLY/MONTHLY/WEEKLY PLAN

Some things you can schedule in a few minutes. Your dreams, however, take a little more time and thought to plan out. That's why I encourage everyone I coach to set aside regular planning sessions for setting goals, breaking them down into action steps and timeframes, and scheduling those steps into their yearly calendar.

The best way I've found to do this yearly planning is to take a retreat. It can be by yourself or with someone whom you trust to bounce ideas off of, such as a best friend or a spouse. At a retreat, you can do more than just identify your goals for the year. You can dig into the details of what it will take to accomplish them and map out what needs to happen in each quarter, month, week, and day of your year. Once you have this done, I recommend taking a day or mini-retreat every quarter to schedule out your action steps for that goal. Each quarter, you'll be able to make adjustments based on what happened the previous quarter. If you blew past your minimum goal last quarter, maybe this quarter you can increase your goals; if you didn't meet your minimum, you'll want to create a plan to catch up.

I also recommend taking at least half a day every month to sit down and schedule the month ahead. Think about what needs to get done during that month to keep you on pace to hit your goals for that quarter. You can do the same thing for an hour every week and for five minutes every morning to plan out your day. Are you seeing the pattern here?

The point with all these scheduling sessions is that you're

making your goals a true priority. You're not just listing your dreams and hoping that they happen for you one day. You're creating space for those goals to manifest in your life through incremental action. The more often you sit down to think through your schedule, the more you can compare each day/week/month/quarter to the one that came before it. You can reflect on what went well, create a plan around the obstacles you foresee, and identify the areas of opportunity to do better next time.

No idea how to go through a five-minute planning session for your day? It's a lot simpler than you might think. I literally sit down with my tea and recite my schedule out loud: "I'm going to have breakfast, then I'm going to drive to work. When I get to work, I'm going to spend fifteen minutes on email and answer only the urgent ones. At 9:15, I'm going to give the staff a ten-minute warning about our meeting at 9:30," and so on. Speaking your daily action items out loud lets your brain absorb exactly what you want for your day. This helps you get those items done. It's incredible how much stress and uncertainty this five-minute intention setting can eliminate, and how much it can boost your productivity.

CLARITY IS THE KEY

I used to collaborate frequently with a head of career services at a major university in Miami. She and I worked with many of her students, helping them advance in school as well as in their careers. She knew I balanced a lot of different things and spent a good amount pursuing my traveling dreams. One day, she pulled me aside to ask how I got it all done.

She shared that she constantly felt anxious and stressed out—not only in her job, but also in her life. She looked at me traveling the world, running seminars, attending conferences, impacting kids, and wondered how I kept it all together. In her eyes, I did five times more than she did, but she felt five times more stress. Our conversation ended with her asking to "job shadow" me for a day.

I'll admit, it was a bit of a bizarre experience having her come to my office and watch me work, especially because I was in my mid-twenties, and she was in her early forties. But she showed up early at my office and watched as I spent the first few minutes of my day looking through my schedule, then called my staff in to walk them through what their responsibilities and goals were for the day and finished up with my usual encouragement: "Let's go kick butt today!"

Later, that head of career services told me she was most impressed by the simple act of me sitting down to look at my day as a whole. She told me she was always thinking about the next activity she had to do. It had never crossed her mind to look at the whole day at one time before she got started.

Think you don't have enough time to spend planning your day, week, or month? Step back and think about how much time you spend in a day/week/month scrolling through social media. Statistically, every American spends a minimum of 10 minutes a day scrolling through their feed. Most people spend three times that long. You have the time. It's simply a question of whether you choose to spend it in a way that gets you closer to your goal.

She also admired the way I walked my staff through the same process, making it clear what I wanted each of them to accomplish. To her, our office's efficiency all stemmed from that amazing clarity and focus. Nobody got sidetracked by random projects or wondered what they were supposed to be working on. She realized that she often gave her staff "busy work" to keep them occupied instead of focused, goal-oriented tasks that kept them moving in a productive direction. She realized that creating daily objectives and weekly goals could be a game changer for her staff.

BE RESILIENT

Planning and scheduling make the path to your goals incredibly easy to follow. But it's important to know that the execution isn't always a simple matter. Even with the best system in the world, you're going to encounter obstacles. Some of them will come from the outside. These include rejection, resistance, or lack of response. Some of those obstacles will come from inside you. These include laziness, loneliness, or just feeling "not in the mood."

A lot of people take obstacles to heart and allow these to prevent them from getting to where they want to be. When a task seems more challenging than you expected, it's easy to start second-guessing yourself. You might start to think you're not meant to accomplish that goal, or you're not truly capable of it.

Those thoughts and feelings are totally normal. The key is having a plan for how to deal with them. I've come to the conclusion that obstacles are designed to test your determination and commitment. Your resilience in the face of obstacles is the proof of how badly you want to accomplish a goal.

I've said it before and I'll say it again: if accomplishing our goals were easy, everyone would be super successful. The most successful people are also the most resilient. Not only do they have a plan in place, but they also know that plan won't always go exactly how they want it to, and they are quick to find new routes to get to the same destination.

On any given day, you might be golden and going down the right path, or you might need to reroute and take a detour to deal with certain obstacles. Some days, you may have lots of free time, while other days the phone won't stop ringing or the kids won't stop screaming. Take the opportunity to reflect whenever your schedule permits, and if it doesn't happen today, schedule a little extra time to make it happen tomorrow.

SCHEDULE TIME TO REFLECT

Personally, mornings are my best time to find a little quiet time for myself. All I have to do is wake up five or ten minutes earlier than usual. For others, the evenings after everyone has settled down or gone to bed are the best opportunity. Maybe for you, it's a lunch break, or even the time you spend in your car commuting.

Whenever you find time, it's important to take some time to reflect on how you've spent your time in the past twenty-four hours. Celebrate your wins and identify where you might need to play catch up. Consider where your areas of opportunity are and ask yourself where you can be more efficient.

As you reflect, make notes of your thoughts. That way, the next day you'll have a clear vision on how to make adjustments. Every time you write thoughts down, these sink deeper into your subconscious mind. Doing this also helps you get to know yourself better. You understand the patterns of your actions, whether these are positive or negative.

The more aware you become about what's happening in your daily life, the more you're able to repeat a positive pattern. Be intentional about this. If you find a positive pattern, intentionally repeat it. By the same token, if you identify negative patterns, think about how you can shift and adjust them. If you repeatedly assess and the positive and negative patterns you identify and constantly adjust as necessary with your overall goal in mind, you'll get to the place you want to go.

I feel confident in saying that the more you make time for this planning process, the more you will start to love it (or at least the results of it). You'll feel the satisfaction of seeing your productivity go up and your stress go down. You'll experience the reward that comes from following through on your commitment.

Don't forget—you don't have to plan all by yourself! Reaching out for help from others can make the planning process more fun and more productive.

But most of all, you'll connect in a powerful way to the "why" behind your goals. After all, planning equals the life of your dreams. An hour of planning is an hour of creating your future. It's an hour of bringing your dreams to reality. It's an hour of being able to create the life that you love. Once you give it a meaning, planning becomes exciting.

INACTION HAS CONSEQUENCES

When you have something that you want to do, you've got to have accountability in order to get it done. It's crucial to know why you're doing something, but you also need to set yourself up for success. You can also have outside accountability, either from a coach, friends, family, or a support group.

I belong to an accountability group that sets consequences if people don't accomplish one of the goals they've set. These consequences are anything but slaps on the wrist. For example, one of the guys in the group had challenged himself to start writing thank-you cards throughout the year, with the goal of increasing his sense of gratitude and getting into a more positive mindset. He pledged that if he didn't follow through by writing five thank-you cards every day for the rest of the year, he'd donate $100 to charity. Another guy challenged that pledge—he told him to donate $1,000 if he didn't get it done. The argument was that if the first guy would donate $100 to charity anyway, it wouldn't hurt him to not do it. If he was truly serious about accomplishing that goal, he needed something to really light a fire under him.

As humans, we psychologically do more to avoid pain than to gain pleasure. This means people are likely to work harder to avoid something they don't want than work toward something they do. The ideal is to have a healthy balance between these two, because they are both good drivers.

You don't always have to set up a penalty for not accomplishing your goals. Sometimes, it's enough to simply recall the "why" of your goal and then imagine the opposite.

In our coaching sessions, Chris and I dived deep, looking at all the reasons why these actions items were important things that mattered to him. Then I asked him to tell me what would happen if he didn't execute the actions he'd scheduled. The answers were right in front of him. He would be exactly like the people around him who were living paycheck to paycheck. He'd still be in a two-bedroom apartment with eight people. He'd end up working for minimum wage and be under somebody else's control. He would lack the freedom he wanted and remain stuck on the same path for the rest of his life.

Most people I coach come to me because they want more. They want to do more, have more opportunities, and create more for their future families. But others come to me because they're in dark places, and they're desperate to get out. They'll only get out of those dark places if they make changes and take action.

Sometimes it's worth thinking about the worst-case

scenario. If you continue as you are and change nothing about your situation, where could this lead you?

LIGHTS, CAMERA, ACTION

Most people think they have to put in time to get some-where: one year to lose the baby weight, five years to earn their first major promotion, ten years to get good at a new skill, etc. In actuality, that thinking misses the mark. Goals don't require a set number of years to achieve them. Achieving your goals doesn't take a certain amount of time; it takes a certain amount of action. Most goals can be achieved in any timeframe you want. Just know that the sooner you want to achieve it, the harder you're going to have to work.

It's incredible how this mental shift sets you free from self-limiting beliefs around your goals. Before 2006, I'd always had the secret goal of performing at a level that no one in my division and only a small percentage of company managers in the country had reached. But I assumed this wouldn't be possible for someone like me, who was only in her first full year as a manager. When I compared myself to the more successful people in the company, I concluded that I would need at least five years to get to their level.

My company's first big breakthrough happened when we

doubled our annual sales from half a million to a million dollars. I remember thinking before we started that this was a big goal, even for me. I actually sat down with a great friend and mentor to ask if he thought two years was too short a time for us to sell a million dollars' worth of product.

He said to me, "Why not do it by next year?"

It was like being nineteen all over again. My friend insisted that I was capable of way more than I thought I was. All I had to do was break it down. Together, we broke the million-dollar milestone down into how many sales reps I'd need and the average productivity per representative. Using these numbers, we created goals for three sales campaigns: fall, spring, and summer. We also set goals for how many people I'd need to sign up for each sales training seminar in order to have a good plan for recruitment. The next question was where to find candidates. We looked at the response rate of different advertising sources, such as newspaper ads and Craigslist, and came up with a plan for outreach. By recruiting five prospects per day, five days per week, I could get 100 new sales reps on my team and have the manpower to push toward the million-dollar mark.

With all these goals broken down into steps, all we had to do was map out the day-by-day execution. Of course, implementing required that I put in more hard work and more dedication than ever before. I'm talking about work that went well beyond just what I did in the office. My goal's success depended largely on the strength of the team I was able to build, and that strength depended on my influence as a manager. I took my personal education and improvement into high gear, spending at least thirty minutes per day reading books, listening to audio seminars, and learning from successful people's experiences in order to accelerate my growth.

This incredibly audacious goal ended up being incredibly simple to execute, and we ended the year surpassing our million-dollar goal, increasing our annual sales quota by over 100%.

This success did more than make company history. It changed the belief structure of our entire staff. Every year after that, instead of asking ourselves what was reasonable or possible, we asked what we wanted to sell that year. All we needed to do was identify what the goal would take, to see if we were willing to commit to the task at hand. If everyone was on board, we would break the goal down into the smallest action steps, identify when they were getting done weekly, and consistently execute those action steps.

Breaking that sales barrier helped me break through a

mental barrier. It turned out that I didn't need years of experience to accomplish something no one in my division had before. All this involved was setting a goal for myself, breaking down the steps it required, and committing to carrying those actions out. I realized I could do anything I wanted as long as I knew the actions it would take and committed to those actions. This got me thinking about the bigger things that were possible in my life.

Marcus White, the successful entrepreneur I discussed in chapter 5, has this great quote: "The harder you work, the luckier you get." Even if you aren't talented at something, if you have a great work ethic and positive attitude, you can create so much more in your life than someone who has a natural aptitude but doesn't put any time into it.

It also made me more discerning about the goals that I set my sights on, and this has continued to inform my work and goal-setting to this day. At this point in my life, I know that achieving a goal means committing to the hard work required. If I'm not committed to the work that a goal will take, I'll readjust. There have been many times when I've chosen to let go of things I've wanted to do because they would take more time and effort than I was able or willing to commit. I trust myself to know when something isn't important to me—if I'm not willing to commit and be consistent, I know it's not the right goal for me to pursue right now.

It's incredibly important to be real with yourself when considering your goals. It's pointless to fill your schedule with action steps toward a goal that doesn't mean much to you. Even with the most meaningful goal in the world, you're going to have great days, average days, and bad days. This makes it extra important to remember your "why" through every step of the process.

I'll be honest with you, I struggled a lot before deciding to write the book you're now holding in your hands. Along with the time I spend running my existing companies, coaching clients, and traveling around the country to participate, lead, or speak at events and seminars, I'm currently embarking on a new business venture with my husband. I knew how important it was to write this book, but I had to really understand the hours and the work that would be required of me.

My husband and I sat down together to break it all down: the work involved for the book along with the work we'd be putting into this new business. Once we had the breakdown in front of us, we spent time honestly searching our hearts about whether it was worth all the time and effort. Was it worth giving up all our free time for the next several months? Was it worth taking other goals off the table? Was it worth braving the hard days that were bound to come?

Ultimately, we decided that it absolutely was worth it.

Success in business means setting ourselves up for the next chapter of our lives (coming soon, we pray) with children of our own. Having the time, money, and flexibility to raise our family while continuing to travel the world if we choose to! Success with the book means empowering others to achieve what they believed was impossible and to create a life they love.

Both goals come down to our ultimate *why* of wanting to leave a legacy. We want our kids, grandkids, and great grandkids to see that our lives were defined by the desire to impact others and help people. We wrote this goal down to govern all the other goals we consider. We only take on the things that will keep us aligned with this goal and help move us closer to it.

Design Exercise

Using the breakdown of your one-year goal from the last chapter, plug each of the actions you listed into your calendar.

Activity: _____

Day/Time: _____

Notes: _____

Activity: _____

Day/Time: _____

Notes: _____

Activity: _____

Day/Time: _____

Notes: _____

Activity: _____

Day/Time: _____

Notes: _____

Activity: _____

Day/Time: _____

Notes: _____

CHAPTER 8

Scare the Crap out of Yourself

People will do more to avoid to pain than they will do to gain pleasure.

TONY ROBBINS

I've attended Tony Robbins' "Unleash the Power Within" seminar three times, and each time, I still get chills when he goes through the "Dickens Process."

You're probably familiar with the story of Ebenezer Scrooge in Charles Dickens' *A Christmas Carol*—how Scrooge, not the nicest person in the world, is visited by three ghosts who force him to review the negative path of his life. The final ghost takes Scrooge into the future and lets him see how he will come to the end of his life being lost, lonely, and miserable. This sad image scares the crap out of Scrooge. He realizes that if he doesn't make changes in his present, that's where he will end up. When the ghost returns Scrooge to the present, he immediately sets to work correcting his mistakes, changing his life today in order to change the course of his future.

Tony challenged the audience to imagine ourselves in that same position. He asked,

"What would your future look like in ten years if you kept repeating negative old patterns? How about twenty years from now...what would happen if you didn't make any changes? Who would be around? Would anyone be around?"

Tony urged us to fully feel the pain of being in that future scenario. He was right—it was a painful process, but effective. I felt every part of my being say, "No way! Change must happen NOW!"

This illustration never fails to bring powerful responses from the audience. I remember one year, a man in the audience stood up afterward to share his struggle with cigarettes. For years he'd wanted to quit smoking, he said, but even as his health issues had piled up, he had never taken action on this goal. He didn't do this until he thought through the Dickens process and realized that if he kept smoking, he wouldn't be there for his daughter as she grew up. He wouldn't be there to walk her down the aisle when she got married. He wouldn't be able to hold his grandchildren. He realized that he wanted those experiences more than anything in the world, even more than he wanted to avoid the challenges of quitting smoking. The pain of potentially missing out on his daughter's life motivated him to take action.

This illustration resonated deeply for me, as well, but in a different way. I was taken back to a situation from my past, one that involved a choice I couldn't change, something I've only shared with a few people prior to writing this book.

I was twenty years old and engaged to a guy who had some serious issues. I didn't realize the depth of the issues he had until after I shared the news with him that I'm about to share with you.

In October of 2003, I found out that I was pregnant, and was shocked at the sudden turn my life had just taken. I remember debating whether to tell my parents or just run off to a far-off country and raise the baby on my own. I wasn't sure how my fiancé would feel, but I knew kids were not in his plan for a while. When I told him about it, there was absolutely no support. I remember him yelling with fury, "You have an abortion, or I'll beat it out of you!" In that moment, feeling trapped and afraid, abortion seemed like the easiest way out. So that's what I did.

It was a dark chapter of my life. Even after ending the pregnancy and breaking up with the guy, I harbored tremendous guilt and regret. For me, having this abortion went against my beliefs and I felt like a hypocrite. More than anything, I wanted to be a person whom my parents could be proud of, an example my siblings could look up to, and I'd made a choice that was completely out of alignment with our upbringing. It was something I felt that I could never share with anyone.

For the first year, that secret preyed on me constantly; eventually, I was able to bury it in the back of my mind, though it always resurfaced (especially on Mother's Day and on what would have been the baby's birthday). I realized later that it prevented me from feeling fully connected in my relationships—I never felt like people fully knew me, because of this shameful part of me that I felt I had to keep hidden.

We think things happen in the past stay in the past, but if we don't deal with them, they keep coming back to affect our lives. Often, they manifest in parts of our lives where we would never have expected them to come up.

Tony's story about Scrooge, and the thought exercise that followed it, made me realize that if I didn't fully forgive myself, I'd never find the true intimacy and connection I desired in a relationship. By not letting people fully know me, I was preventing anyone from fully loving me. I saw myself twenty to thirty years from then, alone, crying, without a partner who deeply loved me, without the family I desperately wanted. The pain of that future was greater than the pain of reopening that episode in my life, dealing with the wounds it caused, and experiencing closure through forgiving myself. I couldn't change the choice I'd made in the past, but I could change the pattern of guilt, regret, and believing I was unlovable.

NOTHING CHANGES UNTIL YOU TAKE ACTION

Tony's illustration drives home the point that goal achievement is a more than a matter of psychology. Making a plan and scheduling your goals is key, but none of it means anything until you do the things in your plan.

Taking action is usually the hardest part of any plan. Sometimes, the only way to push yourself forward is to take a long, uncomfortable look at your worst-case scenario. Ask yourself what could happen to you if you don't take the necessary actions. Let it scare you. Sometimes the only way to overcome your fear of changing is to harness your fear of what will happen if you don't.

Right before I joined Vector when I was nineteen, I
remember thinking about how much it would take to
get to London. Even though I was used to working hard,
I was intimidated by all the planning, the effort, and the
sacrifices I'd have to make. Part of me whispered, *Why
even bother?*

It was a good question, so I thought it through. I thought
beyond the fun adventure of crossing the "pond" for the
first time and exploring a foreign city. If I didn't commit to
my plan to accomplish this goal, would I ever get another
chance to see the world? If I didn't get this credit on my

college resume, what would my job options look like in the future? Would I be able to set myself up for someday having a great job with a good income and travel opportunities, or would I end up like many I had seen, struggling and stressed over money?

That was a future I definitely didn't want. It scared me even more than the thought of extra hard work and sacrifice. But what really pushed me was thinking of the example I'd be setting for my family. I really wanted to show my siblings that if they really put their mind and actions toward something, they could do it!

BREAKING THE MOLD

I've told the story of how I started working at Vector to fund a study-abroad semester in London. What I didn't mention was that even imagining that goal in the first place was an incredible challenge for me.

My family's constant struggles with money had a severely limiting effect on our dreams. My siblings and I assumed that because we didn't grow up in a wealthy, entrepreneurial family with resources, opportunities, and connections, there were certain things in life that we just couldn't achieve.

Don't get me wrong—my parents never discouraged hard

work or big dreams. It was more the people around us who influenced our limited thinking. All around us, we got the message that we should just do the best with the resources we'd been given, and not to raise our sights too high. But that first summer of working at Vector introduced me to concepts I'd never heard of before, including personal growth and development. I started to realize that anything was possible for me if I just broke down my goals and committed to taking action on them. And the more I learned about this, the more I wanted to expose my siblings to the same concepts.

In my family, talking about money was something you just didn't do. It only got brought up when people were crying, fighting, or worrying. But at work, everyone talked about money in a completely different way. It wasn't good or bad—it was just a necessary part of the bigger goals we set for ourselves. By talking about it openly, we were able to deal with it confidently and use it to fuel our dreams.

I knew that this new mindset could change the course of my family's history, but only if I was brave enough to take action on it. I wasn't sure how they would respond to me when I broke the mold by setting my sights on big goals and dealing with money in a new way. But then I thought about what might happen to my siblings if I didn't set the example for them. I imagined them with families of their own, living paycheck to paycheck and arguing over the stress of not being able to provide the life they wanted for their kids. I imagined them without the time or resources to see God's beautiful world and being resentful at me for not sharing what I had learned. This vision of the future scared me more than a possible negative reaction from my family. From that day, I made it my mission to model this new mindset to my family and show them what was possible.

Just as I'd feared, not all of them were happy to see this change at first. My brother in particular was very upset with me for leaving home to attend college. To him, it felt like I was abandoning the family. His anger continued even after I finished school and began working to open my first business. "You were always my role model," he said to me, "and then you just left. Why aren't you here? Why aren't you at home?"

I said, "I want to create a different life." I tried to explain my dream of being an entrepreneur—that having my own business would mean no limits on my earning potential, making my own schedule, being able to travel the world. What's more, I told him, I wanted to show him that the same things were possible for him. He could have any life he wanted if he committed to working hard in order to get it.

As time went on, I started to see my example paying off. My siblings saw me working hard to achieve my dreams, and they began pursuing dreams of their own. My youngest sister was the first of the Vazquez kids to buy a home—a huge feat for someone in our family—and has worked her way up the corporate ladder in her industry. My late sister got her master's degree and was almost done with her Ph.D. at the time of her accident—she was ready to be the first "Dr. Vazquez" in our family.

My brother not only accomplished his dream of becoming a firefighter but has also received the quickest promotions of anyone in his station. He's begun to travel the world as well, taking trips to Spain and Scotland with his wife. He also owns his own home and is learning how to invest in real estate. He and his wife even have a vision board now, which they use to set goals for every year.

With each dream he accomplished, my brother thanked me for opening his eyes to the fact that he could create any kind of life he wanted. It's amazing for me to see everything my siblings have accomplished through their big dreams and hard work, and it's equally amazing to realize that I helped that happen through my example. By overcoming my fear of negativity and rejection, I was able to help shift the mindset of my entire family.

GAIN THE MUSCLE

The strength to accomplish your dreams doesn't come all

at once. In order to gain the "muscle" you need to achieve your goals, you need to do things outside your comfort zone. For me, this meant not only developing skills at my job, but also having the courage to use those skills in full view of my family.

You can't do the same things you've always done and expect different results. If you want a different life than the one you have now, you have to take different actions from the ones you're used to taking.

Pause + Reflect

What is one simple step you could take today to move in the direction of your best life?

For many people, the first step in a new direction is the scariest one to take. Even though they desperately want their lives to look different, the fear of the unknown can be enough to hold them back from ever getting started.

If this is where you find yourself, the Dickens process is a simple but effective way to work through those fears. Sit down by yourself and think through the worst-case scenario that could result from you doing nothing. Imagine every possible negative outcome from making this change, and write them all down.

This can lead to some dark places, but don't shy away from them. If nothing changes, and your life goes in the same direction, what might happen as a result? Will you lose your home? Will your partner leave you? Will your children grow up at risk and impoverished? Will your health get so bad that you can't recover? Will you wake up at seventy years old and realize that you're miserable and alone?

Once you have those worst-case outcomes down on paper, take a long, hard look at them and ask yourself: Would you be all right with those things happening to you? Are you fine with your worst-case scenario being a possibility in your life?

If you're not, it's time to take action. Create a lifestyle where your worst-case scenarios aren't even an option.

Some people refuse to look at the worst-case possibilities of the way they live. They say it's needlessly negative. As a result, they keep going the way they are, and when the undesired outcomes show up, they say they never saw it coming. Considering your worst-case scenario is a good reality check. It helps you make sure that your life turns out in the way you choose.

MAKE THE DANG PHONE CALL

My coaching client Rebecca began working with me after starting a job in real estate. In one of our first conversations, she told me she had a hard time being motivated to reach out to people and follow up with her leads. While she loved showing houses, she hated and feared getting rejected.

In that case, I told her, sales was a funny choice of profession. Sales is a numbers game, and rejection is just a natural part of those numbers.

I asked Rebecca to envision her worst-case scenario if she didn't make the sales calls. The answer was easy: she wouldn't sell any houses. "And if you didn't sell any houses," I asked, "would that be okay? Does it really matter whether you close any sales at all?"

Some people could have honestly answered that no, it didn't matter. If she had a rich spouse paying the bills, for example, there was no reason for her to worry about whether or not she closed on any homes. But that wasn't the case for this client. She did need to close some sales, because she needed the money. She'd taken the job in the first place in order to make enough in commissions to pay her own mortgage.

"Why is that important?" I asked.

At first, she was confused. Why did her mortgage matter? Because she had three boys and she needed to make sure that they had a roof over their heads.

"What if they didn't have a roof over their heads?" I asked her.

She paused for a minute. "Well...we'd be homeless," she finally answered.

"And does that matter?"

"Yes!" she insisted.

"Then make a dang phone call," I said.

Once Rebecca could see the connection between making sales calls and supporting her boys, everything changed. Before long, it became about more than simply paying her mortgage. She started asking herself whether she was fine with not saving enough money for her boys' college tuition, and whether she was fine with them working minimum-wage jobs and possibly having to worry about money their entire lives. Of course, she wasn't fine with that, either. She started seeing sales calls not as an unpleasant task, but as a vehicle to create an incredible life for her family—one they could pass on to their own kids one day. Every time she made a phone call, she was taking action on the goal that mattered most to her.

I asked her how many calls a day were worth making, if making them meant creating the life of her dreams. She settled on twenty calls per day, and even wrote it on a piece of paper that she hung over her desk: *20 Calls Per Day = Life of My Dreams*. She programmed the calls into her schedule and every day, she worked through them. Before long, she was selling an average of one home per month; it quickly increased to two or three per month. By the next year, she was making a six-figure income from her commissions. What's more, her attitude about sales calls completely reversed. She went from dreading rejection to not caring who said no to her. She saw those phone calls as her means to creating the life of her dreams.

Watching people shift their mentality is possibly the best part of my job as a coach. And it all starts with connecting your daily actions to the future you want. If you're okay with your worst-case scenario unfolding in your life, then don't change a thing. But if you have a dream in mind—an amazing, fulfilling life that you'd love to create—then it's time to take action.

Believe it or not, every individual action you take has a deeper meaning than it seems today. Every experience and circumstance are integral parts of your bigger picture. You have the opportunity to create the life you want. It's up to you to make it a masterpiece.

Design Exercise

It's important to remind yourself that each action matters. Using the actions you listed from the last chapter, ask:

- What would it cost me not to execute it?
  - Why does that matter?
  - Why is this important to me?

Put this reminder where you can see it, and let it guide your actions throughout each day.

Action:_____

Cost of not executing:

_____

Why it matters:

_____

Why it's important:

_____

Action:_____

Cost of not executing:

_____

Why it matters:

_____

Why it's important:

_____

Action:_____

Cost of not executing:

_____

Why it matters:

_____

Why it's important:

_____

Action:_____

Cost of not executing:

_____

Why it matters:

_____

Why it's important:

_____

Action:_____

Cost of not executing:

_____

Why it matters:

_____

Why it's important:

_____

PART THREE

Your Success

There's no heavier burden than unfulfilled potential.

CHARLES SCHULZ

CHAPTER 9

Create the Right Conditions

Change is inevitable, growth is optional.

JOHN MAXWELL

Jessie stood out to me from the day I met her. She had a smile that could light up a room and a personality that radiated warm, wonderful energy. Strangely, however, she shone as brightly as she could only in moments that were few and far between. Most of the time, she kept her head down and spoke with no confidence, like she was carrying around some tremendous sadness inside her.

One day, I asked her if we could have a conversation. She agreed, and I told her right away that I saw her as a smart young woman with an incredibly beautiful soul who was filled with potential. I also told her that I'd noticed she seemed depressed most of the time, as though something was always troubling her. If she was willing to open up and share with me, I said, I would love to coach her in overcoming whatever she was struggling with and help her tap into the happy, carefree, joyful person I knew was inside her.

Jessie started to cry. She thanked me for what I'd said. It wasn't often that she heard genuine compliments, she told me. Jessie was used to guys telling her she was hot in order to hook up with her, but no one ever told her she was smart or had great potential. She always had a very low self-image and felt as though she wasn't going to accomplish anything great with her life.

This surprised me, and I asked her what made her think of herself that way. She answered honestly: it had started with her dad. She'd been a very curious kid, always asking questions, and this irritated her father. He told her straight to her face that she was dumb for having to ask so many questions. He added that it wasn't important for her to understand things anyway; she was a girl, so she'd never need to worry about being smart. All she had to do was look pretty. This message was reinforced by a conversation Jessie overheard between her parents. Her dad told her mom that Jessie didn't have a lot of brains, but at least she could get by on her good looks.

Jessie absorbed this message from her father and stopped trying to understand things. As she got older, whenever she wanted something, she would use her beauty to get it. This became more of a problem as she got older. The verbal abuse she'd grown up around combined with the lack of love and connection in her home made her desperate for close relationships, and the only way she knew to get them was by presenting herself in a certain way to guys. Because of her low self-worth, she ended up in one bad relationship after another, sometimes even suffering from physical abuse. She felt embarrassed and mad that she'd given herself away, but she also never felt confident in pushing herself to do more. She hated what her life had become, but she didn't know what to do about it.

I shed tears of my own as Jessie shared her story. But I heard more than just sadness in her voice. I heard frustration. When she finished by saying that she didn't even know what she was capable of, I told her that it sounded to me like she was experiencing a battle in her subconscious. She knew that the way she was living now was not only unhappy, but out of alignment with who she really was. She knew deep down that her dad was wrong, that she was smart, capable, and ready to work hard for what she wanted. The only reason she wasn't living up to her potential was because she didn't know how—no one had ever told her that she had the power to do anything she wanted.

I told Jessie that she brought so much beauty into the

world and that she deserved to be happy and live a life she loved. More than that, I said, she was capable of creating that life for herself. The only question was whether she was willing to go through a process to learn how. It wouldn't all be easy, I told her. There would be sacrifices involved—time, effort, and pushing herself outside of her comfort zone. Did she want to change her life badly enough to go through those challenges?

Yes, Jessie said. She was ready to be happy.

THE RIGHT CONDITIONS TO GROW

After talking with Jessie some more, I learned that her grandmother was a passionate gardener; spending time with her grandmother had given Jessie a love for growing things. The seed metaphor we talked about in chapter 1 resonated very deeply for her. I reminded her that for a seed to grow, it needs to be surrounded by the right conditions—the right environment of climate, sunlight, and soil, along with nourishment in the form of water and careful tending.

In Jessie's case, environment was the first thing she needed to work on. For the past several years, she had surrounded herself with people who didn't show a lot of value for her or for themselves. For example, she belonged to a college sorority where the overwhelming focus was on image. The girls she spent time with were more concerned with superficial matters such as their looks than they were with their grades or potential careers; their main activities, Jessie said, were gossiping and eating disorders. All this had rubbed off on Jessie, making her even more unhappy and conflicted about who she really was.

I told Jessie she needed to get out of that environment quickly and find some new friends who would uplift and support her. It warmed my heart to hear her say that this was exactly what had drawn her to our company. She said working here was an experience unlike any she'd ever had—the environment was so positive, and everyone was so encouraging. When she was at the office, she felt unstoppable. (I had noticed that she hung out at the office a lot, even when she wasn't on the clock.)

While Jessie could control what friends she spent time with, she couldn't change her family or their negative attitude toward her. However, she could create new meaning around her interactions with them, beginning with her dad. I told Jessie that from what I'd heard about him, her dad had some deep internal issues that he was taking out on Jessie. There was no reason for her to accept his words as being the truth about her.

During our coaching sessions, I asked Jessie to write out

all the positive attributes she knew she had. I told her to disregard anything her dad or anyone else had said about her—I wanted her to dig down for the truth that was inside her.

Pause + Reflect

What is something you love about yourself?
(You're allowed to write more than one thing!)

To get her started, I told her that I considered her to be extremely smart. Our conversations had shown me that she had a brilliant entrepreneurial mind. She wasn't oriented toward numbers, but rather toward incredibly creative ideas, and that was a talent she definitely shouldn't let go to waste.

After listing many of her good inner qualities, Jessie wrote out the things she wanted to do, experience, and feel. This exercise forced her to think about who she wanted to be. I remember that in those initial days, very few of her goals had to do with material signs of success. Instead, she wanted to achieve inner peace, experience self-love, and find fulfillment in the things she did. That was a great place for her to start.

With those goals down on paper, Jessie and I put together processes that she could follow to overcome her struggles and create the conditions that would support her growth. To escape the negative environment of her parents' home, she could stay at her best friend's house more often. Instead of hanging out with her sorority sisters, she could spend time at the office, even when she wasn't working. In both situations, she'd be surrounded by people who cared about her and supported the transformations she wanted to make.

Finally, we talked about ways Jessie could nourish her potential. One important way was changing her internal language. Her thinking had been programmed from an early age to belittle herself—to believe she was stupid and incapable. She needed to learn how to battle the inner voices that told her, "You're not smart enough. You're not going to amount to anything. The only thing you have to rely on are your looks."

We created a series of affirming mantras that Jessie could use every time she faced negativity or felt self-doubt. Whenever she heard one of those inner voices telling her she wasn't smart enough to do something, she would follow the same process: take a deep breath and say, "Actually, I'm really smart. I'm very capable. I get straight As in school. I can figure out anything I put my mind to. I have a brilliant creative mind that comes up with amazing ideas and brings out the best in people."

So many studies[23] have shown that the human brain has more negative thoughts than positive ones. That's why your subconscious mind is more likely to constantly replay the negative thoughts and self-doubt you've felt since you were young than it is to help you with positive, constructive thoughts. This is why it's important to talk to yourself more than you listen to yourself. Remind yourself what a badass you are, what you've accomplished, and how many people love and care about you. The more you talk to yourself in a positive way, the less you'll hear the negative.

Every morning, Jessie would stand up straight in front of the mirror, look at herself with a big smile, and read those affirmations. She would also go over her list of dreams and goals, so that she was grounded in the life she wanted to have. Once she had reminded herself of how incredible she was and all that she wanted to accomplish, she'd be ready to connect with people and make an impact.

2   Rick Hanson, Ph.D. "Confronting the Negativity Bias." RickHanson.net. https://www.rickhanson.net/how-your-brain-makes-you-easily-intimidated/

3   Hara Estroff Marano. "Our Brain's Negative Bias." *Psychology Today*. June 20, 2003. https://www.psychologytoday.com/us/articles/200306/our-brains-negative-bias

Remember Marcus White, the successful entrepreneur from chapter 5? He told me that reprogramming his inner dialogue was the number-one most influential factor in his success. He took the lessons from the "Power of the Inner Winner" audio tapes he received in the car lot many years earlier and used them to create a new "internal tape" for himself. He started by reciting things he heard in the tape; as they became engrained into his being, he made a habit of speaking out loud who he was and what he wanted to accomplish each day. This process, he said, was completely transformational.

Pause + Reflect

Stop and write down a few affirmations (declarative statements) about how great you are. You might find your subconscious mind challenging you, saying, "No you're not." Don't let it discourage you—sometimes it takes time for these statements to feel fully authentic.

To make it easier, here's a ninja trick: instead of just stating "I am _____", say "What can I do today to be more _____?" Then you'll always feel aligned with what you are saying!

In the years since our coaching sessions, Jessie has started her own business. She started it with an idea that not many people believed in at first, but she persevered through their negativity with confidence and belief in herself. This idea won her a number of competitions at her university and has gone on to bring her a series of accolades—I've even seen her on the news. When we last got together, she was in tears, thanking me for changing her life. She said she didn't know if she'd even be alive if it wasn't for the new group of people she started surrounding herself with. She was so grateful that she'd become aware of how much the people around her mattered.

Jessie's story proves that, regardless of the environment you find yourself in, you don't have to remain stuck there. You have the power to change your circumstances and create the conditions where your potential can thrive. There are amazing people, coaches, and programs which exist to help you connect with like-minded people. Ultimately, you're the one in charge of designing your life and fulfilling your goals, and part of this is making sure that you're in the right environment for growth. Ask yourself whether you're surrounded by people and conditions that serve you or stand in your way.

Not every environment is good for everyone, just as not every seed can grow under the same conditions. An apple tree needs a very different climate from a cactus, along with different amounts of water, sunlight, and care. The environment that best suits you depends on what you want to do and where you want to go. If you're taking action on your goals, but things aren't working out for you, that doesn't mean you're not capable of accomplishing your dreams. It probably means you need to find an environment that better suits your personality and goals.

GET THE ENERGY RIGHT

In the past, I thought I could muscle my way through any action I needed to take, out of sheer drive. But over time, I realized that there were times when I just couldn't seem to perform at the level I wanted to. I would find myself worrying over small things, getting upset easily, and mysteriously unable to function at my best.

I noticed the same thing in people I coached. They were smart, capable, and had great resources and opportunities, but sometimes they just wouldn't apply themselves enough to succeed. It finally dawned on me that the problem wasn't just a lack of motivation, or even discipline. The problem was energy.

Energy is the fuel of life. If your abilities, talents, and willpower are the car, your goal is the destination, your choices are the GPS, and energy is the gas in your tank. As that energy gets low, no matter how much you have to offer, your progress is going to slow to a standstill.

That's why these people I coached could have all kinds of great resources at their disposal—connections, opportunities, talents, a clear vision, and a sense of purpose—and still not achieve their goals. Their energy was being drained by deep-seated internal struggles. Some had emotional wounds that they'd never recovered from. Some had mental struggles with depression, anxiety, fear, or self-doubt. Some were dealing with chronic health issues. And some were dealing with a lack of inner peace or trust.

Your overall energy is influenced in four different areas, all of which combine to influence the way you go through your day.

PHYSICAL

- Physical energy is impacted by good nutrition, adequate exercise, adequate sleep, deep breathing, and a number of other factors. For many people, physical energy is the foundation of all the others. If we fail to take care of our physical selves, it's much harder for us to master our other energies.

EMOTIONAL

- Emotional energy has to do with the overall direction of your feelings, as well as your mood, your relationships, and your approach to managing conflict and negativity. Low emotional energy contributes to depression and hopelessness, making you want to stay inside and pull the covers over your head even when nothing's really wrong. In contrast, having strong emotional energy gives you an optimistic outlook and an eagerness to live your life, even on bad days.

MENTAL

- Mental energy is a lot less about your IQ and more about your focus, insight, and clarity. You can be the smartest, most educated person in the world, but if your mind is all over the place, jumping from one idea or thought to another, it's going to dramatically reduce your energy to understand and accomplish the tasks in front of you. The most productive people I know are the ones who have abundant mental energy. They can instantly translate an audacious goal into a broken-down list of action steps and help everyone understand exactly what makes each step important.

SPIRITUAL

- Spiritual energy comes from fostering a deeper connection with what's happening around you. This can come through organized religion, personal faith, or simply looking for the greater meaning in the people you meet and the circumstances you encounter. You don't have to believe in God to strengthen your belief system. People who believe everything is random and nothing really matters tend to have a lot less overall energy for their daily lives than those who believe that there's something greater than ourselves giving us all an important purpose in this world.

Depending on your background, personality, and a lot of

other factors, you may be disposed to one kind of energy more than another. The great news is that different energies can balance each other out. For example, I'm fueled mainly by my physical energy—if my body is functioning well, it improves my mood, balances my emotions, and makes me feel great about life. My grandmother, on the other hand, is fueled mainly by her spiritual energy—her strong faith and spiritual practices motivate her to take care of her body, think positive thoughts, and pour out love to her family.

Whenever you're creating something in your life, you want to have the highest level of energy possible. And the conditions in which you exist play a big role in either building your energy or taking it down. Think about it: if you're living in a home where people are constantly fighting, holding themselves distant, or actively tearing you down, all your emotional energy is being used up trying to protect you from those influences. No wonder Jessie, who lived in a home like that, felt sad and depressed most of the time.

By finding the right conditions, you can build all four areas of your energy back up, ensuring that you have the fuel to power your dreams forward. Throughout the process of taking action on your goals, it's crucial to stop, assess your energy, and ask yourself how you can create the conditions that will foster the success you desire.

PHYSICAL ENERGY—GET MOVING

Building your physical energy doesn't require spending hours doing CrossFit or running up and down stairs until you pass out. All you really need to do to maximize your physical energy is get moving.

In this day and age, we tend to make exercise a lot more complicated than it needs to be. With so many different types of gyms and workouts, deciding what to do can be overwhelming. So let me make it super easy for you: just find something you enjoy. Exercise is one of those highly individual conditions we talked about earlier—not every type of exercise suits every type of person. Forcing yourself to attend a class or do an activity you hate is a guaranteed way to give up. Instead, find a way to move that you enjoy. Just about any type of movement will bring you countless health benefits in addition to building your physical energy.

Exercise does a lot more than make your body look good in a swimsuit. There are studies4 showing that exercise also contributes to better mental health, reduces stress and anxiety, and improves memory and critical thinking skills. When you exercise, your body releases chemicals called growth factors which enable the growth of new brain and blood cells. Meanwhile, the increased blood flow supplies your brain with oxygen and glucose, the two elements needed to boost brain energy. The bottom line is, when you're working out, you're benefitting your brain just as much as the rest of your body.

EXERCISE

- Personally, I love boxing. It's a great way to combine cardio and strength training. Plus, it gives me an outlet for any tension or frustration I'm carrying around that day. Another type of exercise that offers similar benefits, but in a totally different context, is yoga. Just twenty minutes on my yoga mat leaves me feeling stronger, calmer, and full of energy.

- Although I really don't enjoy the static repetition of weight lifting, my husband loves it. The best example, though, is my eighty-year-old grandma. At that age, most people would probably give themselves a pass when it comes to exercise. But not my grandma. She's

---

4   Lawrence Robinson, Jeanne Segal, Ph.D., Melinda Smith, M.A. "The Mental Health Benefits of Exercise." HelpGuide.org. March, 2018. https://www.helpguide.org/articles/healthy-living/the-mental-health-benefits-of-exercise.htm

all about practicing Zumba. For someone like her who has always loved to dance, this is the perfect exercise. She doesn't even have to go to the gym. She can just watch a Zumba video online or pop in her "Hip Hop Abs" DVD and spend an hour dancing around her living room, not caring a bit if the neighbors get a glimpse and think she's a crazy old lady.

- If you're just getting started, two exercises I highly recommend are swimming and jumping on a trampoline. Both are fun, low-impact, high-circulation activities that are easy to do with little to no skill required.

- Find whatever form of movement works for you and fit in as much movement as you can per day. If you find it difficult to make the time, download one of the many apps out there that guide you through a seven- to fifteen-minute workout. Just these little bursts of movement will do wonders in terms of boosting your energy for the rest of the day.

- You can do even more to maximize your physical energy by getting a professional involved. For some people, that means working with a personal trainer; for others, it means joining a sports league or finding a weekly class they enjoy. Some people really get into working out after joining a fitness community like CrossFit or Orangetheory. All of these are great ways to make exercise more fun and strategic, in addition to holding you accountable.

- If you can do it, I also recommend working with a healthcare practitioner such as a chiropractor, who can help make sure that your body is aligned properly. Our entire physical body, including our nervous systems and organs, is operated through our spine. If our spine is crooked or not aligned, this hurts the ability of our physical body to function at its highest level. A crooked spine can also affect our nerves, which impacts our brain and emotions.

Pause + Reflect

Our bodies need to move! What is a physical activity you'd be willing to do regularly (or try for the first time) to help your body get the exercise it needs?

NUTRITION

To function at the highest possible level, our bodies need the right nutrients. You can exercise as much as you want, but this won't offset the negative effects of bad nutrition.

The majority of your overall wellness is determined by the fuel you put into your body.

I know you've heard it before, but I'm going to say it again: you need to eat real food. This is the best way to ensure that you're getting as many nutrients as possible into your body. And while there are dozens of competing schools of thought around the best, most nourishing way to eat (paleo, Keto, vegetarianism, veganism, etc.), all of them agree on one thing: processed food does nothing good for your body.

- An easy way to eliminate the processed foods from your diet is to stay out of the middle of the grocery store. That's where they tend to keep the packaged foods full of sugar, preservatives, and chemicals. Instead, guide your shopping cart around the outside edges, where you'll find the real food. You know, the kind you can find in nature.

- As you're getting rid of the processed foods, you should also be incorporating more plants into your diet. I can tell you that this was not always easy for me. Even though I knew how nutrient-dense plants are, I didn't exactly get excited by the idea of munching on mouthfuls of spinach. Instead, I started juicing. Not only can you pack tons of nutrients into a single glass, but you can also make veggies taste amazing by combining them with sweet fruits like orange, pineapple, and mango. These days, I take my fuel a step further by mixing my juices with protein to create a delicious, micronutrient-packed smoothie.

> If those fuel-rich smoothies are starting to make your mouth water, visit the Resources section for tips on where to find my favorite high-quality protein and other ways to elevate your nutrition.

- The more plants you consume, the more you'll start to enjoy them. Not only the taste of them, but all the fun ways to fit them into your favorite foods. For example, I love sneaking veggies into my family's diet by spiralizing zucchini, beets, and carrots into "noodles." At first, you might want to boil them for just a couple minutes to soften them. Now, I like to have the noodles raw with a delicious homemade sauce! It's an easy way I can make sure everyone gets tons of nutrients in their meal without ever missing the traditional pasta.

- Another great idea is to substitute plants for dairy. You can find milk and even cheese made out of cashews, almonds, or hemp seed, offering you tons of protein without the fat and lactose of regular milk. And whenever I'm craving a milkshake, I make a smoothie with frozen berries, banana, and avocado. This gives me the rich, creamy texture and sweetness I crave, with way more nutrients included.

- If you need some extra motivation to incorporate

plants into your diet, there's nothing like visiting your local farmers' market to inspire you. The beautiful variety of sights, smells, and tastes is guaranteed to get you excited about finding ways to enjoy all the natural, healthy foods they have to offer.

DETOXIFYING

In this day and age, people's bodies are loaded with more toxins than ever before. They come in our water, our air, the food we eat, the clothes we wear...everything!

Your body has built-in mechanisms for naturally detox-ifying. But the more toxins that have built up inside you, the more energy it takes for your body to fight them off. That's why it's a good idea to take some extra steps to help your body get rid of the waste. Not only will you look and feel better, but you'll prevent disease, strengthen your immune system and—you guessed it—improve your energy.

When a person has a lot of toxins in their system, they start to smell bad. If any of your bodily odors are bad, that means you've got nasty stuff inside of you that's seeping out. An overall detox will give you better breath, better body odor, and better skin, amongst many other benefits.

While there are lots of intensive detox programs out there, there are also plenty of simple things you can do on your own to detoxify. These are a few of my favorites:

- Eating more plants is one of the primary ways to help your body detoxify. The antioxidants contained in fruit and vegetables purify your bloodstream, while the fiber keeps things moving through your colon.
- Drink a lot of water to clean and flush out your system.
- Take regular saunas to sweat out your toxins.
- Exfoliation techniques, such as skin brushing or using oil, not only get rid of dead skin, but also help refresh your circulation.
- Sip on herbal teas and cleansing juices.
- Add colonics and coffee enemas to boost your immune system, fight cancer, treat autoimmune diseases, reduce depression, or increase energy. (Visit the Resources section for a link where you can learn more about the benefits of these treatments.)

Detoxifying can play a big part in weight loss. Several years ago, my friend decided she'd been drinking too much, and asked me to do a liver detox with her. We spent a month drinking cleansing juices and eating only fruits and vegetables, and guess what happened? We ended up losing about five pounds each, without even trying. How cool is that?

Pause + Reflect

What's one thing you could add or subtract from your current diet to elevate how you fuel your body?

EMOTIONAL ENERGY–GET YOUR GLASS FULL

Emotional energy is about joy, fulfillment, happiness of heart, a spirit of positivity. You can't expect to have good emotional energy if you're holding onto grudges, endlessly mourning a loss, or not setting healthy boundaries. Even factors like indecisiveness, guilt, and excessive stress are emotionally draining.

There are several different factors that can impact your emotional well-being. As you'll see, they all come down to your decision about who you want to be—somebody who is constantly angry, upset, and anxious, or somebody who is passionate, loving, inspiring, happy, and playful. It's up to you to create the conditions that make you the person you want to be.

- Self-talk is a simple but powerful way to shift the balance of your emotional energy. What kind of information are you feeding yourself on a daily basis? If you allow your subconscious to speak, it's likely that most of those thoughts will be negative. To counter this negativity, you have to make a conscious effort to speak good, positive thoughts. Literally say them aloud. That way, you're listening to positivity instead of the negativity you have inside. The more you talk to yourself in a positive way, the more you can start reprogramming yourself.

- Think about the quality of your relationships. Are you constantly angry and bickering with the people in your life? Or do you enjoy great conversations and experience mutual support with them? Can you listen to each other and talk through things, or do discussions typically turn into arguments? Are you building each other up or putting each other down?

When my husband and I got married, we committed to being each other's biggest fans. We didn't sign up to tear each other down for the rest of our lives. If we had something to say that we knew would be upsetting for the other person, it was our job to step away and take some time to think about how to say it in a way that would help the other person, not tear them down. We both saw it as our individual responsibility to bring out the best in each other.

- How do you manage conflict? When something bothers you, it's important to depersonalize the situation and explain your feelings calmly rather than overreacting or saying things you don't mean. Consistently doing either of these, particularly without apologizing later, doesn't only damage your relationships—it hurts you by negatively impacting your emotional energy.
- Check in with your mood from time to time. If it's negative or even neutral, ask yourself how you could turn it up a notch or two? Think about the things that make you smile, the things that bring back good memories with positive feelings attached to them. Whether it's putting on a favorite song, taking a walk by the beach, or scrolling through photos from a fantastic vacation, be proactive about making time and space in your day for it.

In the past, I hated waking up in the morning. The sound of my alarm clock instantly put me in a bad mood. Then one day I heard U2's song "It's a Beautiful Day" on my way to work. It instantly took me back to happy times—mornings when my college best friend would wake me up by blasting it before class, rocking out to the song with friends, and warm-ups with my volleyball team as we prepared to dominate tournaments. I just can't help but smile when I hear that song. For that reason, I started using it as my "get ready" song in the morning. It puts me in the best mood, making me feel ready to conquer the world.

- Deep breathing has become my go-to method for improving my emotional state. Whether I'm anxious, stressed, or upset, I've learned that stopping everything and taking several deep breaths brings an immediate and powerful change to my emotional state. (You can find directions for a deep breathing exercise in chapter 12, and a link to more in the Resources section.)

- If you're going through something that challenges you on an emotional level, it's so important to have support. Friends and family are good, but sometimes you need expert help from a coach, mentor, or support group. Never be embarrassed to reach out for this kind of support when you need it. Instead, own the fact that you're putting yourself in an environment that will foster the growth that you want. You won't be showing weakness. Rather, by dealing strategically with whatever you're going through, you'll be showing strength by making an effort to be happier and love your life.

MENTAL ENERGY—GET PRODUCTIVE

Having positive mental energy starts with focusing on positive, productive objectives. When you don't know what you're supposed to do or when it's supposed to get done, it's a lot easier for your mind to jump around from one thing to another, whatever feels the most stimulating or urgent. In contrast, having a defined focus for your mental energy lets your brain do its best work while gaining strength for the future.

- Taking care of your mental energy includes taking the time to plan. Looking at each week and each day can impact your ability to stay mentally focused. Get your schedule and workspace organized so that when you sit down to work or study, you can maximize your mental energy on the task itself, not on figuring out which task you're even supposed to work on.
- I recommended tackling your most important projects first thing in the morning, while your mind is still fresh. Regardless of how much time these take, you want to invest the bulk of your mental energy in your top priorities. As the day goes on, your decision making and productivity fade, which makes it much harder to focus and think critically.
- Constant distraction drains your mental energy. Instead of checking your phone and email every time you get a notification, turn off the ringer and set specific times to check your messages throughout the day. The more you reduce frequent interruptions, the more you can stay focused on specific tasks and the less you have to spend energy refocusing every few minutes.
- As a coach, I talk to a lot of people about chunking. In a way, it's the same as breaking down a goal, except that

chunking is specifically a way to get through a lengthy task. Essentially, it means breaking down the large task into smaller, more manageable tasks that you can complete in twenty to thirty minutes. Between each chunk, take a short, five-minute break to refresh your brain, then get back in the game to tackle the next one. Tackling your tasks this way keeps your mental energy sharp and ensures that you don't get overwhelmed or burn out.

Chunking isn't limited to business. This is a technique top athletes use to help themselves get through long hours of training or, as in my case, a twenty-five minute cardio session. Since I don't love running, it's a lot easier to "trick" myself into getting on the treadmill if I tell myself it's just five minutes, five times. Doing it this way makes the time go by a lot quicker and distracts my brain from feeling fatigued and overwhelmed.

- In his book *The Organized Mind: Thinking Straight in the Age of Information Overload*, Daniel Levitin talks about how our brains are configured to make a certain number of decisions per day. Once we reach that limit, we burn out. We physically can't make any more decisions, regardless of how important they are. That's why it's important to give your brain small, quick breaks throughout the day, and to take time off on a regular basis (weekends, anyone?) so your mind can recharge.

- Change up your routines to keep your mind sharp. The more you stimulate your mind through activities like learning and reading, the more you'll stimulate your productivity. When you engage your brain in things outside your routine, you increase your brain activity, which results in a natural mental energy boost.

FEED YOUR MIND

Maximizing your mental energy involves feeding your mind with new and inspiring information. These days, there's so much in the news that can bring us down and fuel negative thoughts. It's important to balance such news with positive, productive information and ideas.

- Feeding your mind starts as simply as reading a great book. Books give you unlimited access to so many incredible minds, which helps your own mind think of great ideas. If you don't know where to begin, ask the people you look up to what books they recommend.
- Podcasts are one of my favorite ways to feed my mind. They offer endless topics to explore, usually broken up into thirty-minute episodes. They're perfect for feeding your mind while you commute to work, exercise, or even just hang out on the couch. You can ask friends for their favorite podcast recommendations or Google search podcasts on topics that are of interest to you.

- In Brian Tracy's book *Maximum Achievement*, he talks about different factors that can help you reach your full potential. One of the big things he talks about is self-awareness—understanding what has made you the way you are and why you act in a certain way. Gaining this awareness can help you more easily identify the things you struggle with and set proper systems in place to overcome them instead of feeling stuck. There are many great personal growth and development seminars out there that focus on self-awareness. I especially recommend the seminars offered by Tony Robbins, John Maxwell, and the Landmark Forum.
- As you're building your knowledge base through learning, don't forget to spend time on emotional intelligence. Learning how to not just deal with your emotions, but also channel them in an intelligent, productive way, makes you more resilient and strong in the face of adversity. It also gives you insight into why other people act in certain ways, helping you resolve conflict and make smart decisions about relationships.

SPIRITUAL ENERGY—GET CONNECTED

Expanding your spiritual energy starts by connecting with something greater than yourself in a meaningful way. Whether you attend a church service, spend time in meditation in prayer, take a walk in nature, or sit in mindful silence, the goal here is to consciously transcend your feelings and circumstances in a way that fuels your energy.

- One of the simplest and most powerful ways to maximize your spiritual energy is to practice gratitude. There are so many incredible studies on how gratitude supports you emotionally, professionally and socially.[5] [6] Best of all, it doesn't require any specific faith or practice. All you have to do is focus on appreciating all the good things in your life.

Pause + Reflect

List at least three things you're grateful for—things that make your life right now so much better than it would be without them. (You don't have to stop at three!)

---

5   "10 Transformative Benefits of Gratitude." LiveBoldandBloom.com. https://liveboldandbloom.com/10/mindfulness/benefits-of-gratitude

6   "The 31 Benefits of Gratitude You Didn't Know About: How Gratitude Can Change Your Life." HappierHuman.com. http://happierhuman.com/benefits-of-gratitude/

Tony Robbins talks about spending three minutes on gratitude every morning, a practice that I've incorporated into my life and have seen a lot of benefits from. In the morning, try writing down three things you're grateful for. (It doesn't have to be just three.) As you start your day, say a few words about why you're grateful for each of those things, either to someone else or just to yourself. At the end of the night, list three specific things that happened that day, that you are grateful for. These do not have to be big events—I've written down occurrences as simple as someone bringing me a glass of water in the middle of a training seminar.

- Meditation is another spiritual-energy booster. There are lots of formalized ways to practice meditation, but it really all comes down to quieting your mind, noticing the thoughts and feelings that come up, and intentionally selecting what to keep and what to release. As you go through meditation, you experience a new sense of energy and empowerment. There's so much wisdom that can flow through us if we stop, quiet our mind, and listen.

- Mindfulness is similar to meditation in that it teaches you to be aware of what's happening in the present moment. Often, our minds are thinking about so many things at once. You might be having a conversation with somebody and simultaneously thinking about how you have to pick up your kids or what's on your grocery list. As a result, your mind isn't ever fully present in that conversation. But developing mindfulness helps you be fully present in every moment. It makes you aware of your thoughts, feelings, bodily sensations, and surroundings. This awareness helps you understand others and connect with them better, lower your stress, increase your focus, and not be derailed by unexpected circumstances, thoughts, or feelings.

By training yourself to be more mindful, you can build new neural pathways that boost concentration, flexibility, and awareness. How powerful is that? The more aware we are, the better we can connect to the world around us. Visit the Resources section for some great resources on how to start cultivating mindfulness.

CREATE YOUR CONDITIONS

Always remember that you need certain conditions in order to grow into the person you want to be. Think of it this way: you don't throw seeds into a vacant lot full of gravel, trash, and weeds and expect them to become a flourishing garden. Or if, like me, you're not a gardener, here's another way to think of it: you can't pour wine into a dirty wine glass and expect to get the best flavor out of it.

Creating your best conditions requires understanding yourself and the environment that suits you best, and making sure that you incorporate those things into your daily life and practice. You're in charge of creating the energy you need to take actions which will move you in the direction of your dreams.

Even though you're the only one who can decide on and create the conditions for living your best life, it's a lot easier to begin creating those conditions when you have the support of like-minded people. Over the past few years, I've built an amazing community on Facebook called Live Elevated that is focused on providing resources that help people maximize their energy to live the life of their dreams. Visit the Resources section to learn how you can get connected with our community.

Design Exercise

Take a quick look back through the four different types of energy. Based on those categories, what are two things you'd be willing to add or subtract for the next week/month/six months that could increase your energy and accelerate you toward achieving the next best level of you?

CHAPTER 10

Take Care of You

It all begins with you. If you do not care for yourself, you will not be strong enough to care for anything in your life.

LEON BROWN

Back in chapter 3, I told the story of how I spent 2007 working really hard to surpass my sales goal for the year. I was at my peak professionally, but I wasn't fueling my energy in any way. By the end of the summer, I was number one in a quarter-billion-dollar company, but I hated my life.

Initially, I blamed my job for why I felt so terrible. All the things I loved about working there—building relationships, connecting with people, helping others realize their potential—had disappeared into a numbers game. If you had asked me who my top thirty people were that year, I could have told you their names, but I didn't know anything about them as people. I didn't know what goals they were working toward or what their personal dreams were. With the connection to people gone, I no longer felt happy or excited about the work I was doing.

When I mentioned this to my mentor Trent, he was surprised to hear that I was unhappy with my job. He knew how fulfilling I'd always found it and began asking me about my lifestyle. What was I eating on a regular basis? How often was I exercising? What was I doing for fun? When was the last time I'd gone to church?

I told him I didn't have time for any of those things. The only thing I had time or energy to think about was hitting my sales numbers for the year.

"Cathy, there's no wonder you're so drained," he said. He pointed out that I had been thinking exclusively about serving everybody else's needs while completely neglecting my own. If I didn't take care of myself, Trent warned, I'd never be able to serve people at the level I wanted to.

The job wasn't the problem. I was the problem. I wasn't taking the time to do the things that refueled my energy. Working somewhere else wouldn't fix my life. What I truly needed was to reconnect with the things that excited and healed me. Only by prioritizing my own energy could I influence and impact people in the way that I wanted to.

RECONNECTING WITH MY ENERGY

As I mentioned before, I attended a leadership conference shortly after this conversation with Trent. The conference was held at a church, and as my friend Lisa and I approached the entrance, I started to feel nervous. I hadn't been to a church in a long time, partly out of exhaustion from my job, and also partly because I was still dealing with anger over the death of my cousin. Growing up, my spiritual energy had been a powerful source of motivation for me, but at that point in my life, it was practically non-existent.

As soon as we walked inside, though, I immediately felt the presence of a powerful energy in every part of me. As people began singing and dancing, that feeling became so strong that I started to cry. That energy had always been such a big part of my life, but I'd been missing it for so long. That event made me realize how much I needed to take care of myself, and that this started with reconnecting to my spirituality.

I began filling myself up spiritually by reading scripture and journaling. Those practices immediately impacted my emotional energy for the better, and the more positive I felt, the more clearly I was able to think. I saw that if I was going to do all the things I wanted to do, I needed to create a process that would fuel the happiness I needed to be truly productive.

REFUELING MYSELF...AND MY TEAM

My new system started with identifying what I needed to do in order to show up at my best. I used my staff as a motivator: if I didn't take the time to take care of myself, I wouldn't be able to serve my people at the level they deserved.

I began each day with an affirmation. Instead of rushing out the door, I took a minute before leaving the house to look in the mirror and remind myself that I was a badass. Instead of running to the drive-in for lunch, I picked up healthy food and juices from an organic café. And at least once per day, I stepped out of the office, turned off my phone, and refueled my energy with a boxing session or a yoga class.

The more time I spent focusing on programming positive, energy-fueling practices into my life, the better our team performed. The next year, we broke the all-time national record for a summer campaign, in spite of a whole slew of crazy challenges that had never happened before. We got kicked out of our office, forcing us to move the whole business in the middle of our busiest season, lost our phone lines, and our internet didn't get installed until a full month after the move. It was a total mess, and I worked much harder in the summer of 2008 than ever before, but I was undoubtedly happier that year than I'd been in a long time. My team and I were positive, resilient, and able to laugh through the challenges. We were so committed to our goals that there was never a doubt in our minds we would find a way to make things happen.

As the office leader, it was my job to set the example for everyone. The fact that they were able to lift each other up, take initiative in solving problems, and have fun while working their butts off was a direct result of the work I'd done on retraining my priorities.

I remember watching that summer unfold and thinking, more than once, about what a difference a year can make. By focusing on the importance of taking care of myself, I was able to influence those around me and help create an incredible, rewarding summer for everyone.

PUT ON YOUR OWN OXYGEN MASK FIRST

When you're on an airplane, you're instructed to put on your own oxygen mask before helping those around you. It seems counterintuitive, but in order to help other people, you have to be alive and breathing yourself. It might feel like the right thing to do to help someone else survive before looking after yourself, but it's actually not the smart thing to do.

The more you want to do and the more you're trying to cram into your days, months, or years, the more important it is to constantly refuel yourself—there's only so long you can sacrifice yourself before you run out of fuel. And when that happens, the consequences are truly scary![7] You'll become burned out as well as resentful or angry toward others for needing so much from you. However, that anger isn't other people's fault—it's the result of not taking care of yourself.

No matter what kind of relational position you might be in—leading an office, parenting a child, being married, serving as part of a team—you always want to show up at your best for the people who count on you. For women in particular, this often creates a tendency to sacrifice themselves in order to take care of everyone else. Women often say that all they care about is serving their family, but in reality, neglecting themselves only makes them less happy and less effective. It's extremely important for women, as it is for everyone, to make sure that they're filled up so that they're able to continue giving, loving, and supporting the people who matter most to them.

FIND YOUR PEAK

As we've talked about before, everyone has different needs and preferences around how and when their self-

7   Richard Boyd. "Adrenal Fatigue, Chronic Fatigue and the Bodymind Aspects of Burnout Syndromes." EnergeticsInstitute.com, 2015. https://energeticsinstitute.com.au/adrenal-chronic-fatigue-burnout/

care happens. It's up to you to find the conditions that best suit your means of refueling your energy and create rituals and routines that ensure your refueling takes place.

Brian Tracy says, "Successful people have successful habits." Just doing something once or once in a while isn't going to refuel you the way you need. You have to program your habits into your life, so you engage in them easily and automatically. The less you have to think about your refueling opportunities, the more you'll get out of them.

Sometimes, the conditions that best serve us require we change our current habits. I used to hate getting up early in the morning, but once I discovered the magic of listening to a mood-improving song (U2's "Beautiful Day," remember?), I've found that mornings are my best time to get stuff done. My motivation to give mornings another try came from a friend, mentor, and former colleague at Vector, Hal Elrod, who is now better known as the founder of the Miracle Morning community and author of a book called *The Miracle Morning: The Not-So-Obvious Secret Guaranteed to Transform Your Life (Before 8AM)*.

Hal writes that he went through a tough time during which he wasn't on his A-game. Like me, he felt drained, disconnected, like nothing was going right for him. A friend told him something very wise: his level of success would never surpass his level of personal growth.

With that advice in mind, Hal began researching the habits and self-care rituals of the people he admired. He learned that the most successful people were fueled by things like journaling, exercising, affirmations, and visualization. Hal wrote down everything he learned and turned it into an acronym that helped him get his life back on track. This simple formula has now also helped transform the lives of millions of people across hundreds of countries!

THE LIFE-SAVING ACRONYM: SAVERS

S IS FOR SILENCE.

Silence includes any sort of mindfulness practice—prayer, meditation, or just deep breathing. The most successful people are those who take time to stop, pause, and breathe. It's such a gift to pause and take time to connect with either yourself or God. Doing this sets you up for your day in a way that nothing else can.

A IS FOR AFFIRMATION.

It's not a coincidence that the most famous celebrities and top athletes are vocal about affirmations, visualizations, and positive thinking along their journey to success. Successful people often talk about how they visualized what they wanted. For example, Jim Carrey wrote a check to himself for the film salary he would earn one day.

Muhammed Ali constantly told himself (and everyone who would listen), "I'm the greatest ever."

Affirmations remind you of what you're capable of and what you can do, but their real power is in being spoken out loud. By speaking the words out loud, you're reprograming your inner self to become who you want to be. The more you feed your mind positive thoughts, your actions will align with these.

When creating your affirmations, identify what you really want, why you want it, whom you are committed to being in order to get it, and what you are doing to obtain it. You can include inspirational quotes and philosophies. If you're stuck for ideas, search for sample affirmations online. There are so many out there for increasing energy, having great relationships, developing self-confidence, building wealth, or losing weight.

Pause + Reflect

List one or two simple affirmations that have come to mind since chapter 9. It doesn't have to be long-winded or profound—just think of statements that you would like to embody or remind your subconscious of when you find yourself focusing on old patterns or negative thoughts.

V IS FOR VISUALIZATION.

A lot of people don't believe in visualization, but there's so much science[8] [9] [10] which suggests that our brains don't know the difference between what's real and what's not. For decades, this practice has been used among high

8   David R. Hamilton, Ph.D., "Visualisation Alters the Brain & Body." DrDavidHamilton.com. April 19, 2011. http://drdavidhamilton.com/visualisation-alters-the-brain-body/

9   Jim Lohr, "Can Visualizing Your Body Doing Something Help You Learn to Do It Better?" ScientificAmerican.com. https://www.scientificamerican.com/article/can-visualizing-your-body-doing-something-help-you-learn-to-do-it-better/

10   Emilie Pelletier, "4 Scientific Reasons Why Visualization Will Increase Your Chances to Succeed." Entrepreneurs.Maqtoob.com. https://entrepreneurs.maqtoob.com/4-scientific-reasons-why-visualization-will-increase-your-chances-to-succeed-5515ef2dbdb7

achieving athletes. Research shows that in many cases mental practice is almost as effective as actual physical practice. In a study[11] conducted on Soviet athletes from the 1970s, they found that the athletes with twenty-five percent physical training and seventy-five percent mental training were more prepared than those with one hundred percent physical training. When we see things, even in our imagination, our brain feels them.

Try it out for yourself. Think about a moment when you accomplished something amazing. Let your brain focus. What happened? Where were you? How were you standing? Who was around? How were you smiling? How did it feel to have accomplished that?

Create a picture for yourself of everything that happened, allowing yourself to feel anything that comes up—take a second to close your eyes and try it. (Seriously—take a second!) Did you notice yourself starting to feel happy and proud? You're not even in that moment and yet, because you've seen it in your mind, you start feeling the positive feelings associated with that moment.

The same happens with a negative memory. If you think of a time when you were sad, such as a time of loss or frustration, you'll start feeling those negative emotions in your body.

---

11   Logan Christopher, "The History, Science and How-To of Visualization." BreakingMuscle.com. https://breakingmuscle.com/fitness/the-history-science-and-how-to-of-visualization

Visualize something like buying a house for your mom or taking your family on an incredible vacation that they've always dreamed of. Picture the looks on the faces of your loved ones; imagine them jumping up and down with excitement and calling their friends with the good news. Once you visualize how incredible that would feel, your mind and body can't wait to take action. It's almost like you've hypnotized yourself to think about those things.

As soon as you open your eyes, your mind and body feel ready to take on the day. Not only does your mind know what it's working for, but it also knows how good it's going to feel when you get to that end result. That way, you're able to propel yourself to get there so much quicker.

E IS FOR EXERCISE.

There are endless benefits of exercising, but you must find something that works for you. Many people say they don't exercise because they're too busy or they are just exhausted, but I have found that people are pretty good at making time for things that are fun or important to them. As we talked about back in chapter 9 my first recommendation is to find something you enjoy so that you *want* to do it! Next, start thinking of exercise as the way to obtain the physical fuel you need to achieve your goals. Do you want to run around with your grandkids? Climb a mountain? Have more self-confidence? Be more focused?

Whatever it is you want to accomplish, exercise can help prep your mind, body, and spirit to be in the best state to accomplish it.

R IS FOR READING.

We've talked already about how the most successful people spend time feeding their minds and expanding their knowledge. The more you learn, the more success you earn...and this doesn't only have to do with money. You can learn through reading how to be wealthy in joy and love, how to succeed more as a better parent, how to grow closer to God, how to perform a new skill. The list goes on and on. Reading can help you become a better person and a better leader.

S IS FOR SCRIBING.

Scribing is just another word for writing stuff down. We've talked about how important it is to write down goals, but Hal advises taking that to the next step with journaling, another technique used by most successful people. Personally, I find journaling especially helpful in practicing gratitude, but it's also a good way to help you evaluate your life, your dreams, your goals, and the breakdowns of each goal. You can use your journal to celebrate the things that went well for you, building positive emotions that help propel positive actions. Journaling also helps you gain clarity by emptying your mind. Whenever you feel like you have a lot going on, write it down on paper—you might be surprised what comes out.

Along with all of its other benefits, scribing (or journaling) is a strategic way to avoid overwhelm and process emotions. I discovered this after Trent, my mentor, sent me a Jim Rohn journal that came with a CD about how to journal. At first, I was self-conscious about it—was I supposed to write "Dear Diary" at the beginning of every entry? However, as I practiced it each day, I realized how helpful it was to capture ideas, sift through my thoughts, process emotions, and gain clarity that ultimately helped me create better plans of action.

Later on, it also occurred to me that the thoughts I captured in my journals could be helpful for generations to come. Maybe that isn't the case for you. You may write certain things which you never want anyone to read. In that case, you can burn them. But regardless of whether you end up keeping your journals, it's therapeutic to get your thoughts out of your head and body, and onto the page, where you can do whatever you want with them.

STAY STRONG

Sometimes people do things to fill their tank, and these actually end up depleting them. We all know people who love going out to party all night, people who indulge in certain substances that affect their ability to make good decisions, people who can spend hours zoning out in front of the TV or the internet.

While these things might seem to refuel them by helping them relax or forget their stress, they actually have the opposite effect, especially over time. When you stay up all night, chances are you won't be able to sustain the levels of energy you need to fuel your success the next day. Absorbing too much of the content that's prevalent on TV or the web has the opposite effect of feeding your mind, causing negative thoughts and emotions that hold you back.

Be intentional about the activities you engage in to feel happy and bring yourself energy. Do these serve your goals by properly fueling your energy, or do they drain energy away and make you incapable of carrying out all that you want to do?

If you have chronic problems such as addictions or abuses, or you find your mental patterns really difficult to break, don't be embarrassed to seek out professional help. Although some people regard others as weak when they turn to a professional for help, in my opinion, those who seek help are stronger than those who don't. It's a brave decision to want to be at your best and realize that you can't get there on your own. By getting help, you're letting your pride down. You're being stronger than your own ego.

HAPPINESS LOVES COMPANY

While self-care is important, you don't have to do it by yourself. Find people who can support you on your journey and help get you to where you need to be.

I advise people to think of their self-care routine the same way they would think about their hygiene. Could you go days without a shower? Technically, you could, but it wouldn't be ideal. By making a daily practice out of fueling yourself mentally, emotionally, spiritually, and physically, you'll be able to go into every new day feeling fresh and replenished.

Whatever you do choose to do to take care of yourself, make sure it works for you. No matter what habits and rituals you set for yourself, you don't have to be strict with the time you spend on each step. The most important thing is to create a routine which serves you and that you know will help fuel your energy.

Design Exercise

Identify three things you can do daily, weekly,
or monthly to take care of you!

CHAPTER 11

Find the Tribe That Lifts You Up

You are the average of the five people you spend the most time with.

JIM ROHN

In 2005, I joined a group of Vector managers on an incentive trip to Cabo San Lucas. One night, a group hangout in the hot tub developed into one of those conversations that becomes deep and powerful without anyone realizing it. It went from talking about the books we were reading to where we wanted to travel to our professional and personal goals for the year.

As we were talking, Jon Vroman, who was our national sales promotion manager, pointed out how cool and unique it was to have this type of conversation, and how it was only possible because of the caliber of people involved. (Jon went on to be a senior trainer for Tony Robbins and is now the founder of Front Row Foundation.) Because we were all goal-oriented, driven to be our very best, and eager to support each other, it made these deep, searching conversations easy.

Jon told us to think about the top five people we spend the most time with and identify whether these were people who moved us forward or held us back. He also cautioned us that nobody—family, friend, loved one, coworker—could truly be neutral. If someone wasn't actively engaged in supporting our desire to be our best, they were pulling us backward.

To protect our energy, he said, we had to be intentional about not only how we spent our time, but also with whom we spent it. Jon warned us that most people have the tendency to give their time to whomever asks for it. If we wanted to achieve our goals, we all had to think about whether we were giving our time primarily to people who gave back to us or to people who only wanted to take from us.

BEWARE OF THE TIME VAMPIRES

Before this conversation with Jon, I'd never really paid attention to the people I was spending time with. Jon helped open my eyes. I realized that I only have a certain number of hours in the day and a limited amount of energy. I asked myself, who was I giving that energy to? Was I spending time with people who multiplied my energy or sucked it away?

I don't remember if Jon said it this way, or if I came up with this idea on my own later. But as I started considering the various people in my life, the ones I gave my time and energy to, I started thinking of a few of them as "time vampires." These were the people who complained and focused on the problems in their lives but did nothing to seek out opportunities to make things better for themselves. Just being around these people was exhausting for me; however, I had never considered the effect that exhaustion had on my growth as a person.

With this new perspective, I was able to also identify the givers in my life. Not only did they understand and support my goals to create a life that I loved, but they had similar goals for themselves—even if they didn't know it yet. Their positivity and love for life pulled the best out of me. Every time I hung out with them, I left feeling inspired and full of energy.

That conversation with Jon opened my eyes to the idea that I can choose the people I spend the most time with. In fact, it's my responsibility to choose those people wisely. If I wanted to become a better person in every area of my life, I had to make sure I was spending time with people who gave me the energy and positivity I needed to make that happen.

This was a total paradigm shift for me, and I remember talking with a friend about it later. I shared what Jon had said with her, and told her that I wanted to be intentional about who I spent my time with. Everyone is always moving backwards or forwards, I told her, either green and growing, or brown and dying. And the people we spend our time with have a big influence on which direction we move in.

It wasn't a coincidence that this particular friend was, at that time, dating a guy who was bringing her down. She had always been a happy, upbeat person, but during the months of their relationship, his negativity and pessimism had changed her. She'd lost a lot of her great energy; she didn't seem like her full self, and I was worried for her. Even though her boyfriend wasn't actively abusive toward her, he didn't care about growing himself or learning to communicate effectively. If she had the idea to go out and have an adventure or to attend a seminar on personal growth, he complained about it and tried to persuade her to stay home with him and do nothing. As a result, she wasn't doing any of the things that were truly important to her. She realized for the first time that by not lifting her up, he was pulling her down.

While there are some people you should probably cut out of your life, you don't have to completely sever ties with everyone whose negative energy brings you down. There are times where you simply can't avoid being around these people—they might work in your office or show up to every family gathering. When that happens, just be intentional about limiting your time with that person, and make sure you refuel yourself afterwards by doing something that reenergizes you, or having a quality conversation with someone who helps you be in your best state.

THE GIVERS

Jon's words kept ringing in my ears, even after I'd returned home from the Cabo trip. I sat down one day and made a list of all the people I spent time with on a regular basis. The list was divided into two columns: the givers and the takers.

The first column identified the people who brought me to life and made me want to be better. An obvious person was my grandma. A beautiful soul with endless amounts of compassion and patience, I've always wanted to be just like her. Throughout my life, I would take any chance I had to spend time with her, even if it was just for a few minutes. My dad, grandfather, and his sister (my Titi Nellie Ann) were also at the top of that list—they are selfless people who pour continuous support and love into my life. My soul is so much happier every time I am with them!

Two other people on my list were my friends Lisa and Kelly, whom I'd known since college. These women have such powerful positive energy that I can actually feel a change in my physical state when I'm around them. Their smiles and laughter bring joy to anyone around them. In addition, they have an incredible spiritual connection to a higher power—anytime I am going through something difficult, I go to Lisa and Kelly and ask them to pray for my situation. Every time I go home to Florida, I make sure to spend time with them. Even a short visit with them never fails to move me forward in my life personally, professionally, and spiritually.

Another two on that list were Rachel and Simcha, Vector colleagues who also had been part of the hot tub conversation in Cabo. Hanging out together that night had made us really good friends. It was bittersweet to say farewell when they moved to Israel. Anyone who knows these two beautiful souls would agree that they bring such life to the people around them. They constantly pour into people, telling them what they love and admire about them. Even just their smiles light up the room. Again, I only get to see them every few years or so, but every trip refuels me through incredible conversations, ideas, and general catch-up. They're people I love being around, so I make every effort to spend time with them.

Along with being a good friend, Rachel was one of the top female sales associates in Vector Marketing history. I wanted to learn how to be a top seller, so I went to watch Rachel during my training. She took me under her wing, spending a lot of time helping me tap into my potential. Jon had talked about workplace relationships as well—that even in the office, we can choose which relationships to invest most of our time in. It all came down to the small decisions, Jon explained. If Jon was on the phone with a random person and saw a call waiting from one of the top five people on his "giver" list, he would interrupt the first conversation and pick up the call from his top five. In any given day, he had only so much time for conversations. That's why he prioritized the opportunities to talk with people who refueled him, pushed him forward, and radiated positive energy. The best use of Jon's time was receiving energy from these people in order to bring out the best in himself.

I knew that for me, no matter who else I might be talking to, I would gladly end the call to talk with Jon, Rachel, or Lisa. In the limited time that I have each day, I want to spend as much of it as possible around the people I admire. I want to be asked how I'm feeling physically and spiritually, and I want to be challenged about what I'm doing to grow myself and my business. I also want to hear them share great things about their own lives. It's not just because it feels good. It's because I want their positive characteristics to rub off on me.

Pause + Reflect

List the people who lift you up the most.

THE TAKERS

It proved to be a lot harder to list people on the taker side. Like most people, I didn't surround myself with malicious or obviously harmful people. I could point to a number of people who weren't actively tearing me down, but at the same time, showed no interest in growing as people or creating a life they loved.

Even neutral people can be takers. These are the people who make it easy to settle, whether in a marriage, a friendship, or a family dynamic. Being around them is neither harmful nor joyful—it's just comfortable. While there's nothing wrong with being comfortable around someone, you have to ask yourself whether spending a lot of time with this type of person helps you or holds you back. Do you aspire to be like these people? Do they believe in you or help you believe in yourself? Does their influence rub off on you in a way that improves your progress toward your goals, or does your motivation seem to disappear after spending time with them?

The bottom line for my list wasn't whether the people were nice, meant well, or were close to me. The only question was whether or not being with them gave me more energy or drained it away.

In my mid-twenties, I had to add a close family member to this list. I understand that part of being a family is sometimes showing the worst side of yourself, and it was hard to categorize someone in my own family as a taker. However, this person had become particularly selfish and self-absorbed; as a result, most conversations with her were very negative, and interacting with her had become extremely draining for me.

It was really hard when I had to communicate how I felt to this person, but I had to have the conversation in order to set the boundary. I told her that I loved her, but I wouldn't be able to spend a lot of time around her anymore if she continued to act and speak to me in the way she generally did. While I wanted her to be in my life, I didn't want the constant arguing and negativity our interactions usually involved. In the future, I told her, we would probably be talking less, and anytime our conversations went against my morals or my sense of what was good, I would have to end the interaction. I explained that it wasn't because I didn't care about her, but rather because her behavior brought out the worst version of myself, and I wanted to be the best I could be.

Since that time, I've had to have this conversation with a few different people, whether it's because they have done things to harm me—lie, steal, constantly complain—or because they've simply brought out the worst in me and said things that didn't align with my beliefs. It has always been a difficult thing to do, because of the love I've had for these people. But it's precisely because of that love that I've thought it was so important to tell them the reasons behind the boundary I was setting.

I coached someone who was struggling with a parent. For years, their relationship had been bad, even nonexistent, but now the parent wanted to get back into my client's life. He was constantly getting calls from his parent asking him to go and do all of these different things. The son felt obligated to give his parent a chance, but at the same time, he wasn't sure it was something he really wanted.

I counseled my client to set boundaries that prioritized his own comfort level. He didn't have to go to the parent's house or let them come to his house. He didn't have to spend the whole day with them or commit to regular get-togethers. Instead, he could say he was open to meeting up once a week for coffee or a meal. They could start by catching up once a week for an hour, and after that brief meeting, he could assess how he felt. If his energy was positive afterward, it might be a good sign to spend more time with that parent in the future. If he felt upset, guilty, or anxious, he owed it to himself to limit the time he spent with them.

If you have to limit the time you spend with someone whom you're close to, I recommend identifying and communicating the things you love about them but explaining that interacting with them stands in the way of you being the best person you can be. Explain how you want to focus on improving as a person, developing your relationship dynamics, mental toughness, and patience. It's within your right to want to be a better human and to create a life you love, and if someone expects you to spend time with them, they need to understand the role they play in making your life better or worse.

Personally, I like to see the best in the world and the best in other people. I am definitely far from perfect, and I'm sure there is someone reading this whose energy I've drained at some point, but I pride myself on being able to bring out the best in others and want to be around people who do the same thing. If someone isn't interested in doing that, I know that it isn't serving me (or them) to invest too much time in that relationship.

Pause + Reflect

List a few people whom you should probably limit your time with.

CIRCLE OF INFLUENCE

Author Jim Rohn once said that a person is the average of the five people they spend the most time with. These are the people whose mood and beliefs influence your emotional and spiritual energy; the activities you engage in when you're with them have an effect on your physical energy; the conversations you have with them feed your mental energy. As you spend time with them, you'll inevitably begin focusing on whatever they are focusing on, aligning your beliefs with theirs.

That's why it's imperative to be clear about whom you're giving your time to. Ask yourself: Who are you having the most conversations with? Who takes up most of your time? Do you aspire to be like these people? Do you want them around when you're striving to be your best self?

We have all heard the saying "birds of a feather flock together." In communities, churches, sororities, fraternities, clubs, etc., the people who dress the same, talk the same, and act the same tend to spend the most time with each other. But it's not always the case that people were similar in these ways before they met. It's just as likely that by spending time with each other, they became more and more alike without even realizing it.

You could leave your circle of influence to chance and circumstance, as many people do. But when you're designing a life that you love, you don't have to take whatever friends come your way. You can be proactive and create a circle of influence full of people you actually want to be like.

There are endless benefits to having a positive circle of influence. You feel more connected, fulfilled, and at peace because you can feel their energy moving you in a positive direction. There's less stress and anxiety because you're not being sucked into a downward spiral of complaining, negativity, and stagnation. Your thinking becomes more positive and creative. You're able to handle conflict better and see more opportunity for your gifts and talents. You're also able to give so much more of your own resources, because the people in your circle are eager to receive from each other and lift each other up.

Often in our lives, we spend a lot of time talking to people who either need our help or need someone to complain to. While wanting to be there for our friends is a good thing, too much time spent helping, listening, and supporting these people can ultimately hurt you. Remember the oxygen mask analogy in the last chapter—if you don't prioritize your self-care, you can't bring the best of yourself to help others. What's more, you can't truly help someone who isn't interested in helping themselves.

In contrast, the more you surround yourself with people you admire and look up to, the more your subconscious will start copycatting that. If you spend time with those people, you will start acting like them. Surround yourself with the people whom you want to be like.

After that conversation in Cabo, I began focusing more than ever on spending more time with the people who really inspired me. Jon himself was one of those people. I remember talking to Jon later on about the organization he created, the Front Row Foundation, which is all about creating magical moments for people with terminal illnesses. He told me his goal was not only to bring joy into the lives of suffering people, but also to inspire those who aren't suffering in this way to be proactive about doing things that fill them with energy. That's why he always finds opportunities to encourage people the way he encouraged our team in Cabo San Lucas to form a positive circle of influence and seek out people who bring them joy and make them want to be a better person.

Throughout my life, Jon's message has been a great reminder for me. Every time I'm inspired by someone, I make it a point to spend more time with them.

Along with reassessing your dreams and goals, it's important to regularly evaluate your circle of influence. Each time you meet someone new or make a new friend, take the opportunity to decide whom you want to spend the majority of your time with. This may change from one year to the next, or even one week to the next, as your needs and circumstances shift. Making these decisions might feel hard to do at first, but setting boundaries is an important aspect of the self-care we talked about in the last chapter.

Personally, I've found that scheduling is a great way to keep these boundaries strong. Maybe you arrange to see certain people once a month, or only a couple of times per year, while others you arrange to spend time with every weekend, or to call every other night. Be intentional!

Some people will always try to push the boundaries you set. Just remember that you don't have to agree to spend time with someone every time they ask. You have the right—as well as the responsibility—to say no if spending time with that person has a negative effect on you.

PROXIMITY IS POWER

As you consider your current circle of influence, you might realize that it needs to be overhauled. If the top five people in your life don't have a positive, empowering, life-affirming impact, it's time to be intentional about surrounding yourself with people who do. The most successful people don't wait for good influences to show up in their lives. They seek out relationships with people they respect and admire. If you don't know a lot of people who offer the kind of influence and energy you want, go out and find them.

This is a lot easier than it sounds. First, identify the *types* of people you want to spend more time with. Next, think about where you can find that time and those people. Then, start showing up. There are also great online communities (Facebook is an easy resource) where you can connect with some incredible people.

Say you dream of being an entrepreneur, but all your friends work nine-to-five jobs that they hate. Go out of your way to attend conferences and business events to meet incredible entrepreneurs. That's where you can start building relationships and having new people in your network.

Maybe you're interested in spending more time in nature because it feeds your soul and gets you physically active. If your friends are mostly interested in spending the weekend playing video games, search online for local meetup groups organized around hiking, bird-watching, or conservation efforts.

Imagine you want to be stronger in your spiritual walk.

It's not going to serve you to spend your time with people who are pessimistic and purposeless or focus more on their doubts than on finding something to believe in. Try visiting a local faith community, whether it's for a worship service or just an informal gathering or event. Even if you don't end up committing to that specific faith, you can start forming relationships with people who will support your journey and keep you accountable.

If your goal is to be in great shape, it's pointless to spend your time with friends who stay home all day eating Cheetos in front of the TV. Start visiting different fitness classes or gyms in your area. Learning a new activity is a great way to make friends, both with experts and with people who are new to it like you.

So many of us grow up in a bubble full of people who are just like us (or who we think we are). As we get older, we tend to stay in that bubble out of comfort, fear of the unknown, or just not knowing that we have the ability to form relationships through intention and choice. Forming your circle with intention is an incredibly powerful way to shape yourself and your life, however you want it to look. In the words of Tony Robbins, "Proximity is power." The more time you spend with people, the more you become like them. Think about what you can do to put yourself in proximity to those who inspire you and whose success you want to emulate.

BECOME ACCOUNTABLE

One of the most powerful effects your circle of influence will have on you is accountability. It starts with their example. Seeing other people's dedication, consistency, and progress will motivate you to do the same. But as you develop these positive relationships, you can begin reaching out to people in your circle directly for the accountability and feedback that will spur you forward.

The system you set up for accountability is really up to you. This is another area where you need to create the best conditions for your personality and needs. Some people can briefly check in with an accountability partner once a week and be good to go. Other people need longer, in-depth conversations, or to have these more on a more frequent basis.

Depending on what type of accountability helps you thrive, it may make sense to sign up for sessions with an expert, such as a fitness coach, a counselor, or a spiritual mentor. This is especially true if you're working on a particularly complex or specific goal. But if all you want is someone to come alongside you in your journey, it's easy to set up accountability with a friend who is moving in the same direction you are.

The point is to set up a system for yourself so the accountability doesn't fall through. Know which groups you're going to participate in, buy your membership and gear, and schedule the meetings into your calendar. Set up a weekly call with a coach or a daily call with an account-ability partner. Making commitments with your time and—especially—your finances is an important part of ensuring your accountability will last.

Even people who have more of a "lone wolf" type of personality will benefit from accountability. I fall into that category myself. I tend to prefer doing things solo rather than in a large group. And because I'm very inter-nally motivated, I can usually get pretty far on my own. However, I've found that being part of high-performing mastermind groups has been extremely beneficial for pushing me past my comfort zone and helping me prog-ress beyond what I thought was possible.

Exercise is a good example. I love working out, and I'm pretty disciplined about making it a part of my schedule. But as my fitness goals have developed, I've realized that I need to incorporate certain activities that aren't as much fun for me—lifting weights and running on a treadmill, for example. With this in mind, I decided to try out the fitness club Orangetheory. The first time I went to the class, I absolutely got my butt kicked. About halfway through the intense workout, I would have been more than happy to quit. But looking around at all the other participants pushing themselves, I felt motivated to push myself. If they could do it, I could do it, too. Without the other students even saying anything, they challenged me to accomplish what I set out to do.

My business is another area where I'm extremely self-motivated. A stimulating conversation with a few colleagues a couple times a year, sharing ideas or current things that are working, is all I need to boost my annual performance. Some of my peers, on the other hand, love having daily communication with colleagues. It serves them well to share what they're doing with one another on a regular basis. For me, that much interaction would be more of a hassle than a help, but I know it's very beneficial for many.

The bottom line is that even if you're not someone who naturally puts themselves out there, there are still opportunities for you to benefit from strategic communication with a positive circle of influence.

FIND WHAT WORKS FOR YOU

Your circle of influence should work in harmony with the other ways in which you feed your energy. For example, one of my clients feeds his mental energy by listening to two instructive and motivational podcasts every morning. He draws strength from hearing affirming words spoken out loud. He follows this up by having a daily check-in with his life coach, either through a five-minute phone call or just a text. Once per week, he has a longer phone call with his coach; once per month, he goes in for a face-to-face session with the coach. For him, speaking his intentions to someone else and then reporting back on how he did motivates him to work harder so he doesn't let that person down. He also attends events and conferences throughout the year, where he can spend quality time around people who are similarly motivated.

This client is extrinsically motivated. His drive is fueled by external factors such as encouragement, praise, and expectations from people who support him. He thrives off talking with others, soliciting their feedback, or even competing with them. Many times, he will do more for others than he will do for himself.

On the other hand, I'm a more intrinsically motivated person. I'm rewarded by my own sense of accomplishment and excellence. While I appreciate encouragement and kind words, I couldn't care less when people try to set goals for me or say things to push and challenge me. I'm driven by beating my best, and my greatest sense of reward comes from accomplishing what I set out to do.

I once had a colleague who would always try to engage me in friendly competition. He'd come up to me and say me he was going to beat my sales for that week. I looked at him like he had three heads. I'm just not wired for competition with others. I like to win, but as I mentioned, I like to beat my personal best.

This colleague ended up finding a daily accountability partner who could engage in the kind of competition he enjoyed. They drive each other to work hard, laugh and talk smack to each other, and consistently surpass all of their goals. Both of them are top managers, just like me. We're just wired differently.

It's important to identify whether you're intrinsically or extrinsically motivated so that you can set up an account-ability system that effectively drives you forward. Imagine if no one were around to notice you at work. Would you put in your greatest effort, or would you get distracted and find excuses? Think about the kind of relationship dynamics that bring out your best work. For some people, friendly competition is a great motivator, while others thrive more on vulnerability and deep discussions. Some people are driven by negative reinforcement; if they're told they can't do something, they'll work twice as hard to prove that they can. Others thrive on praise and encouragement. For these individuals, being noticed and appreciated for the smallest thing launches them into enthusiastic productivity.

Finding out what styles of support motivate different people is one of the reasons I love coaching. Everyone likes to be acknowledged for what they've done well, but everyone has a different way of getting there. As you seek out the right people for your circle of influence, make sure that you're spending time with people whose style of communication and encouragement matches your own.

Design Exercise

Identify the top five "givers" in your life—you know, the people who increase your energy to its highest level—and schedule time to catch up with at least one of them this week. Go ahead and shoot a text real quick to see when they have a minute to speak with you. In fact, I challenge you to connect with more than one.

CHAPTER 12

Don't Give Up

What if everything you're going through right now is preparing you for a dream bigger than you can imagine?

RENAE SAUTER

In Brian Tracy's book *Maximum Achievement*, he tells the story of a man called Clement Stone. This man was known for being an "inverse paranoid." Instead of fearing that the world was out to get him, he believed that everything in his life was conspiring to do him good. No matter what happened to him, he was convinced it would help him in some way—teach him a lesson, move him in the right direction, show him which opportunities to take. When one door closed for him, he knew he was just supposed to go a different way.

Maximum Achievement had a huge influence on me when I read it in 2002, and this inverse paranoia concept was one of the most impactful parts of the book. I'd seen people complain about problems, issues, and setbacks and wonder how they were ever going to get to where they wanted to be. I'd never met someone who, like Clement Stone, saw every difficulty as a challenge meant to enrich him, empower him, or advance his causes. I remember thinking that being convinced that everything that happens is meant to serve you and power you forward was a great way to live your life.

This is a strategy common among successful people. They might not be true "inverse paranoids," but they maintain an attitude of everything happening for a positive reason or offering them a potential lesson. Think about it: if we all went through life expecting the universe to support and guide us, it would be so much easier to see opportunities for success. We could feel much happier and achieve at a much higher level if we saw obstacles as guidance from the universe meant to push us in the direction of our dreams.

FIVE STEPS

No matter how talented you are, how many resources you have, or how well you have crafted your conditions for success, there will be times when you encounter roadblocks on the path to achieving your dreams. Roadblocks can come in the form of practical challenges, relationship conflicts, challenges to your health and well-being, or sudden unfortunate events that you never saw coming. No matter how adversity shows up, how you handle it—mentally, emotionally and practically—will determine how successful you are.

In my coaching practice, I give clients five keys for how to handle adversity.

- The first key is knowing that adversity is just part of the game. You can't avoid it, so it's something you have to expect. In business, relationships, and life generally, things will happen that you didn't expect to. Sometimes, these are things you can't do anything about. There's so much in the world that we can't control, even with the best planning and preparation. If you're fixed on never encountering adversity, it will only feel worse when you experience it.
- The second key is to prepare yourself internally for the things you can't control. Cultivating emotional intelligence, strength, and courage is critical to weathering adversity when it happens. As a firefighter, my brother prepares himself physically and mentally for any possibility. The second he hears a siren go off, he knows he could be about to face an ugly, daunting situation, but he's equipped and ready to go and tackle it. As you progress on the path to your dreams, know that you will face bad people, ugly circumstances,

and confusing decisions. That's why it's imperative to set up processes for yourself to deal intelligently with adversity. If something doesn't go according to your plan, are you going to complain and get angry, or are you going to assess the situation and decide how you can move forward? Pain is inevitable, but suffering is optional.

- The third key is to let adversity teach and strengthen you. This doesn't happen on its own. It involves making a choice in each new situation. In my life, I've encountered tragic events I'd hope no one would have to experience. Each of these situations brought fresh grief and disappointment along with an opportunity to seek new strength and learn a new lesson. Remember: you're never truly alone in your situation. There are so many people out there who have gone through a lot of ugly things, from sexual and physical abuse to the death of a child or a spouse. Far too many of those people get lost in their trauma, and don't see a light at the end of the tunnel. If you choose to learn from your adversity and become stronger, you can be a light for those who see no light. It's a beautiful thing to be the person who reaches out to those who see no hope and pulls them forward.

Mother Theresa once said: "I know God doesn't give us more than we can handle. I just wish he didn't trust me so much." Not everything that happens to us is for a good reason, especially things like unexpected loss or terrible abuse. However, if these things do happen to us, we can choose to grow stronger and help develop others who encounter such difficulties along their journeys.

- The fourth key is to learn from others who have already overcome adversity. I love inspiring stories and hearing how people overcame situations that didn't seem possible. There are so many examples of people who encountered unimaginable obstacles—the kind anyone would assume were impossible to overcome—and found ways to transcend them and transform their lives. Research what those people did to get through their difficulties. Read their autobiographies, listen to their talks, subscribe to their podcasts. Leaning on their inspiration will offer you the hope you need to keep pushing forward.

- Stephen Hawking's life offers proof that people with disabilities can rise to the highest level of the academic world.
- Jim Carrey's story of leaving school at age fifteen to support his family and living out of a van during his early years shows that anyone with talent and drive can make a name and a fortune for themselves.

- Oprah's tragic background of sexual abuse, teen pregnancy, and loss of a child is a testament to the power of creativity and determination to transform your life.
- Bethany Hamilton's surfing career should have been over after her arm was bitten off by a shark. Instead, she went on to win multiple championships in the sport, inspiring countless people along the way.

- The fifth and final key is to enlist support. In life, it always feels good to have encouragement and support, but it becomes crucial when you face adversity. Building a strong, reliable tribe of friends and family will keep you safe and supported when times get tough. They'll remind you of your worth and ensure that you don't lose track of your goals.

TOOLS FOR TRANSFORMING ADVERSITY

One of the most daunting aspects of adversity is the way it messes with your ability to make decisions. The harder the challenge, the harder it is to distinguish between what feels good in the moment and what is genuinely productive for your physical health, mental focus, and emotional and spiritual well-being.

As I always tell my clients, you can't make positive decisions with negative emotions. For instance, if you're in a bad mood, it's unlikely your conflict management skills will be at their best when you sit down for a difficult conversation with your romantic partner. The issues you're trying to resolve will only get worse if you go into the conversation with rage or frustration. A positive outcome depends on being in a positive state of mind.

While some challenges take more time to work through than others, there are a number of ways that can help restore your emotional and mental state to a place where you can make good decisions.

BREATHING

When something goes wrong, when self-doubt creeps in, when a setback interrupts your flow, one of the most powerful things you can do is take deep breaths. This strategy often gets overlooked because it's so simple. But I can tell you from experience that it feels incredible and delivers instant benefits.

You can use this technique anytime, anywhere—whether you're sitting in traffic or locked in a tense conversation with a loved one. All you have to do is inhale deeply through your nose, pause and hold it for a second or two, and then release the breath until it's all gone. Do this however many times you need to until you feel your body calm down. Once your body feels balanced, your mind can think clearly and help you identify what's really going on. (For deep breathing exercises, visit the Resources section.)

STEPPING BACK

I recently spoke to a client who was feeling frustrated by a very challenging situation. He started talking through the situation, blow by blow, until I stopped him midway through and asked what he was actually upset about. It turns out he had layered so many different issues on top of each other, that he had become more frustrated with his own thoughts than with the situation itself. When he actually identified what was making him upset, he realized it wasn't such a big deal after all.

So often, a single setback or conflict sets off an avalanche of negative thoughts and emotions, and this can lead to more conflicts and even more emotions. You have to step away from the situation and identify what is actually happening for you. Forget about all the different details of what happened and ask yourself a few simple questions: What negative feeling are you experiencing? What specifically led to your feeling that way? Will this matter in five years?

This has been very instrumental to calming my emotions in moments of overwhelm, helping me move past things that don't serve me, and in finding solutions to things at hand.

CHANGE YOUR STATE

One of the worst characteristics of adversity is that it can make you feel stuck, like there's no way out. A key part of overcoming adversity is actively changing your state—physically, mentally, and/or emotionally. By activating one of your energies, you'll recharge all of them and recover your positive outlook.

Remember my client Jessie? When she heard voices of self-doubt, her process was to look in the mirror and speak her affirmations. Changing your state can be as simple as changing your self-talk. Challenge the negative voices in your head by speaking positivity out loud. You can also change your state by stepping outside, hitting the gym, or taking a drive to clear your head.

Both my husband and I have found that exercise is super helpful in avoiding conflict in our relationship. For him, going for a run releases frustration and frees up his mind to process situations differently. Personally, running puts me in an even worse mood; instead, I spend some time practicing yoga, which helps me release tension and clears my negative emotions. By the time we both come back from exercising, we are clear about what was actually frustrating us and know what we need to change in order to resolve the conflict between us.

Another highly effective state change happens through music. Everyone has a song that puts a smile on their face, even when they're in a horrible mood. It might make them think of a favorite memory with their friends or a romantic moment with their partner, or simply bring them peace in the midst of chaotic circumstances. Music has the power to transform our emotional state and motivate us to take positive action.

If you're not entirely sure what works for you, test different things out. Try things to see what makes you feel better. It might be that music works for overcoming one situation, while affirmations or exercise help you overcome another.

ADJUST YOUR PLAN

It's all too common for people with big dreams and detailed goals to lose all their determination when adversity strikes. As soon as something goes wrong with their plan, or unexpected setbacks kill their momentum, they freak out, unable to imagine how they'll ever hit their goal now.

Because I coach a lot of people in sales, I often see clients dealing with the crash of a deal they were counting on. For some, this feels like the end of the world. Without that deal, they feel as though they've lost all hope of buying a home, taking that trip, or starting their own business. One of my clients had a certain goal to close a certain number of sales in order to take her family on a much-needed vacation. She had broken down the steps and knew exactly what numbers she needed to hit by the end of the month. But when the month came to an end, one of her sales unexpectedly fell through. She was totally shaken and couldn't face telling her whole family that the vacation was off.

It's great to know the steps required to achieve your goal. However, just because you execute those steps, it doesn't guarantee that everything will go as planned. You might know the exact direction and the exact steps you need to take, but there will always be unexpected occurrences. It's not your job to control everything, but rather to keep in mind exactly where you want to go and find a different way to get there.

When you're on the road, you might sometimes enter an address into your GPS and start along the route only to come across a road closure that just happened, a parade that blocks off a street, or a sinkhole in the highway. I remember when Hurricane Harvey hit Houston in 2017, the overpass to get from the highway to my office was underwater. We literally had to take boats across it because it was impossible to drive.

Adversity doesn't mean you have to change your dreams. It just means you might need to readjust the steps that get you there. If there's something you want badly enough, you're going to find a way to get it, no matter what challenges stand in your way.

Looking back, I can't think of a single time in sixteen years of doing business when I've achieved a goal through the exact plan I originally made. I broke down the steps and took them, but life always managed to throw me curveballs along the way. When those unexpected circumstances showed up, I had to take them in stride and readjust my plan of action. After a while, doing this became completely normal.

Life will throw things at you which you don't expect. Make sure you're flexible enough to readjust your steps to steer yourself back in the right direction.

FORGIVE AND MOVE ON

Human beings can be so loving and supportive of others while being incredibly hard on themselves. Compliments are a great example of this. Think about how often you tell someone they look great; now think about how many times you've looked in the mirror and found something to criticize. It's much easier to be kind and loving to other people than it is to be loving and kind toward yourself.

It's just the same with forgiveness. If you're like me,

when someone else makes an innocent mistake, you're probably great at looking past it and forgiving them. But how willing are you to forgive yourself when you feel you messed up? If you're like most people, you follow up your mistakes with negative self-talk. When you fail or make a mistake, you beat yourself up. When you fall short of achieving your goals, you tell yourself you're not smart, capable, or talented enough.

I can tell you from experience, judging or beating yourself up for "knowing better" or "making a bad choice" will not serve you. It can sabotage future success in your personal or professional life and will hold you back from being able to fully create the life of your dreams.

Unforgiveness is equally unhealthy when you're holding a grudge against someone else. If you find yourself holding back forgiveness, you already know the pain and resentment it creates within you—what you may not know is that it can affect all areas of your life, whether you think it does or not. In order to begin living a life you love, now is the time to make a decision to let go of that old wound.

At the end of the day, we're all human, which means sometimes we're all going to take wrong turns and make bad choices simply because we don't know better. Only robots are designed to do everything perfectly the first time. Humans become perfect by making mistakes and learning from them. Take it from me: even being a really positive person doesn't save you from feeling down sometimes, and coaching other people doesn't mean you have all the answers or get everything right every time.

You have to learn to forgive yourself when you fall short of your own expectations. Beating yourself up is the farthest thing from productive; the only way to move forward is to encourage and support yourself. Instead of punishing yourself, identify the lessons you can learn from every experience. Each can offer you new knowledge and strength, but only if you look for them.

Think of your life as progress, not perfection. As long as you're constantly moving forward in life and striving to get better, you're on the right track. Challenge yourself to find ways to beat your best by next week, next month, or next year.

I was listening to one of Oprah Winfrey's "SuperSoul Sunday" podcasts[12], and the gentleman she was interviewing, author David Brooks, spoke about how when he asks people the question, "What made you *you*?" their answers are almost never positive. He went on to say how no one says, "Oh, that vacation to Hawaii that one time is what built my resilience and drive to succeed." If you do some research, you'll find some pretty incredible stories of overcoming adversity among the most successful people!

Yes, even the most famous, wealthy, and successful people had to overcome some sort of tragedy or endure

---

12   Oprah Winfrey Podcast (November 19, 2017). *Oprah's SuperSoul Conversations—David Brooks: The Road to Character* [Video]. Retrieved August 23, 2018, from https://www.youtube.com/watch?v=UB-t1NvYxbU.

a difficult trial—the kind they wouldn't want anyone else to go through. But these experiences were exactly what drove them to do something incredible, whether it was starting a company that changed an industry, writing a book that became a best-seller, or sharing a message that touched the lives of millions of people around the world.

It's the simple truth that most people aren't inspired to do great things while on a luxurious vacation in Hawaii. It's usually the dark times in our lives that inspire and drive us to do something that makes a difference, whether it be in our own lives or in the world. When you learn to react to negative events in a positive way, amazing things happen.

Design Exercise

What is an old thought or pattern that you know derails you from achieving at your highest level? What is a process you can create for yourself to interrupt that and keep yourself on track toward achieving your dreams?

Example: Getting anxious about a mistake or not hitting a goal.

Process: Pause, take a couple deep breaths, and ask "What can I learn from this?" Remind yourself that there is always a lesson that can serve you! Then ask "What can I do right now to help me move forward?" and take action!

Conclusion

As a young girl, I remember watching my uncle spend hours each day putting together intricate puzzles of five thousand pieces or more. Every time I came over to his house, I would go over to his puzzle table to see how much progress he had made.

One day, I thought I would help him, and grabbed a piece to see if I could position it properly. But as I looked across the table, I remember feeling extremely overwhelmed—I did not have a clue as to where this piece could possibly fit. My uncle patiently watched me as I stared with frustration. Finally I broke the silence, and half yelled, "Where does this even go? How do you know where all these pieces go?"

He smirked, which only frustrated me more. But then, he went on to share some wisdom with me:

"Cathy, puzzles like these take great patience. You don't always know where the pieces belong, but you know that they *do* all belong. Sometimes you grab a piece, but you might not figure out exactly where it fits until way later, and that's okay. You have to learn to enjoy the game. I enjoy the process of thinking, analyzing, strategizing. Eventually, it all unfolds, and you see where every piece fits perfectly to form this beautiful picture."

He pointed to the picture on the front of the box, adding,

"The process develops great strengths that can really help you in life."

At twelve years old, those words did not mean a ton to me. I honestly didn't think about them until about seven years later, when I was trying to console a friend who was suicidal. I remember listening to Nick (what we will call him to protect identity) as he shared some experiences he had been through, painful experiences that seemed to have no meaning or purpose—I couldn't justify why anyone would have to undergo such pain.

As I listened to him, though, I was filled with peace. I remember asking Nick, "Could I share something I just thought about?"

After I received his permission to share, I went on to share my uncle's puzzle story with him, and finished by saying,

"Nick, I feel like every one of us has a beautiful picture that is a portrait of our lives. Every moment and experience we have is a piece of the puzzle. Sometimes it takes a long time to see where those pieces fit, but it's all part of a beautiful masterpiece that is our life. Imagine you're holding a piece of the puzzle, and it's an ugly brown and weird shape. You know the end picture is a beautiful waterfall in the middle of a gorgeous rainforest. As you look at the piece, you think 'There is no way this belongs to this beautiful picture.' I want to challenge you on that, because maybe that piece is part of the scum that's on the rock at the bottom of the waterfall, in the middle of this beautiful portrait that is your life! If that piece was thrown away or left out, the picture would be incomplete and lose its beauty. You'd be focused on the missing piece versus on the rest of the picture."

Nick stayed quiet for a moment and then said, "Wow, I never thought about it like that." We went on to talk about how life throws things as us that we don't understand, but how it's all part of our journey. Nick ended up putting the suicidal thoughts aside, and is now doing incredible things. The puzzle story really resonated with him—it gave him a new lens to look through, just like it did for me.

OWN YOUR PIECES

I always grew up believing that my life was guided by some sort of master plan. I was convinced that while my Creator had a vision for the beautiful masterpiece that my life would become, it wasn't all out of my hands—I got to have a say, choosing colors and making creative decisions.

As my life unfolded, though, some of the pieces didn't seem to match the big picture. Not if the picture was something good, anyway. It wasn't until 2003 that I started to realize that all these pieces really did belong, even the ugly ones. The fact is that there are a lot of hurting people in this world, and as I mentioned earlier, hurting people hurt others. There will also always be the radical people who take actions beyond our comprehension, and circumstances that are out of our control. But while some of the pieces of my puzzle weren't the prettiest colors or the nicest shapes, they were all still part of a beautiful masterpiece that was my life.

We can all choose the meaning we give to what happens. We can all choose to learn or gain strength from every experience and allow it to keep us moving forward in our journey. Even though there may be times when you're handed a piece of your puzzle that might not initially seem to fit, OWN IT! The picture would not be the same without it.

If you are patient and trust that every piece belongs, you

will eventually see it all come together to form a beautiful masterpiece.

That masterpiece is called your life.

CREATE YOUR MASTERPIECE, STEP BY STEP

Throughout this book, we've talked about the steps involved in designing a life you love.

- Realize that no matter what your life has looked like in the past, you have unlimited potential.
- Give yourself the freedom to dream big, without limits or judgment.
- Think about the why behind those dreams, what they represent to you, and what it would mean for you to accomplish them.
- Define your non-negotiable goals. Identify what you're willing to commit to, and focus all your decisions on those things.
- Create timeframes for your goals along with a breakdown of action steps that help you make progress every day.
- Find and create the conditions that contribute to your success.
- Prioritize the self-care rituals and routines that set you up to perform at your best.
- Build a tribe that will lift you up, help you constantly

move in a positive direction, and challenge you to think bigger than you do.

- Never give up. If you have something that you want, you can always find a way to make it happen!

As you embark on this process, I am so excited for you to find out how good it feels to know where you are headed and live each day with intention. Yes, it takes time to accomplish all the goals that contribute to your dream life and, in some ways, the journey of creating that dream life never ends. But simply being engaged in the process transforms your life into something better and bigger than you've ever experienced before. Instead of just getting from one day to the next day, you'll wake up with a new excitement—the kind that only comes from having a direction and a sense of purpose for your life.

You don't have to wait until you get to the big picture to start living a life you love. Once you know exactly what you want your life to look like, your day-to-day activities suddenly have so much more meaning. You can start loving every day, along with every new puzzle piece (experience) that is provided for you.

With every goal you achieve, every dream you cross off your list, you'll find new ones to set for yourself. It's not out of dissatisfaction, but because you love the process of growing, achieving, and succeeding at things you never used to think possible. With each new dream, you can revisit the exercises in this book and find new ways to challenge yourself to go deeper, progress further, and make new plans for bigger and more amazing things. It's the journey that gives meaning to everything you do, so don't ever stop. You never know what things you're capable of until you start with a dream. I pray this excerpt from *A Morning Offering* by John O'Donahue may be true for you:

> ...May I have the courage today to live the life that I would love. To postpone no longer but do at last what I came here for and waste my heart on fear no more.

It's time to go out there and start living a life you love TODAY!

Acknowledgments

First and foremost, thank you to my incredible husband, Spencer Christen. You are the reason this book exists— thank you for pushing me out of my comfort zone and supporting me every step of the way.

Thank you to my family for always encouraging me in my endeavors, even when it meant time away from home. I love you guys so much! Special shout-out to my parents. Mom, thank you for teaching me work ethic and pushing me to be the best leader I could be. Dad, thank you for teaching me unconditional love, being the guiding light in my life, and always standing by my side and being an incredible role model for all of us!

Thank you to my Vector family who forever changed my life. Bruce Goodman, Al Di Leonardo, Dan Casetta, and Loyd Reagan—thank you for being incredible examples of exceptional leadership and providing a killer environment for people to grow! John Kane, Jon Vroman, Trent Booth, and Scott Dennis—your support, love and passion have created ripples that I know will last for generations to come!

Thank you to my friends (new and old). I am so blessed to have the incredible tribe I have had for so many years. I'm not sure there are many people in this world who are as lucky as I am to have such an incredible circle of influence in their lives. Julie and Omari, thank you for always believing in me. Lisa and Kelly, thank you for being prayer warriors for me since our early college days. Andy, Keith, Kattie, and Marielou, you guys are just so freaking amazing and I'm not sure where I'd be without you!

Hal Elrod and Jon Berghoff, thank you for creating a space that made this book possible! If it wasn't for BYEB, I'm not sure this book would currently exist! You guys are rockstars at pushing people to their next level, regardless of where they're at.

Resources

I am a huge believer in continual personal development. I love to read and regularly attend seminars and conferences that challenge my thinking and what's possible. I wanted to share a few of my personal favorites.

BOOKS

Maximum Achievement by Brian Tracy

The Miracle Morning: The Not-So-Obvious Secret Guaranteed to Transform Your Life (Before 8AM) by Hal Elrod

The Four Agreements by Don Miguel Ruiz

Emotional Intelligence 2.0 by Travis Bradberry & Jean Greaves

Get a PhD in You by Julie Reisler

Front Row Factor by Jon Vroman

Seven Levels of Intimacy by Matthew Kelly

How to Win Friends and Influence People by Dale Carnegie

The 5 Levels of Leadership by John C. Maxwell

Think and Grow Rich by Napoleon Hill

Rich Dad, Poor Dad by Robert Kiyosaki

Awaken the Giant Within by Tony Robbins

Unshakeable by Tony Robbins

PERSONAL AND PROFESSIONAL DEVELOPMENT PROGRAMS

The Landmark Forum: http://www.landmarkworldwide.com

Tony Robbins' entire Mastery University is fantastic, but if you can only attend two, I would recommend "Unleash the Power Within" and "Date with Destiny": https://www.tonyrobbins.com/events

Flourishing Leadership Institute's LEAF/AIOS Training:
https://www.lead2flourish.com

Hal Elrod's *Best Year Ever Blueprint:*
https://bestyeareverlive.com

OTHER AWESOME TOOLS

Two apps I love that help with meditation and mindfulness are Insight Timer and Headspace.

The Think Up app is great for building a positive mindset and creating personalized affirmations.

I've created a Facebook community called Live Elevated. It offers free classes on how to increase emotional, mental, physical and/or spiritual energy, plus expert speakers, recipes, motivation, and a great support system of like-minded people committing to maximizing their energy. Join here: http://bit.ly/EFNcommunity

My favorite plant-based protein powder/meal replacement (you can even bake with it) and energy boost can be found at https://www.liveelevatedfn.com/

More information about the benefit of coffee enemas and colonic therapy can be found at the following link: https://www.healthline.com/health/coffee-enema

How to Use a Journal, a guide written by Jim Rohn, was a tremendous help to me when I first started journaling: https://www.amazon.com/How-to-Use-a-Journal/dp/B000HKVTVW

The following link provides some great tools you can use to help reduce stress and anxiety while building mindfulness and inner peace: https://positivepsychologyprogram.com/mindfulness-based-stress-reduction-mbsr/

Let's Connect

I love meeting like-minded people and sharing resources! It is also great to hear from people who have been impacted by reading my book or hearing me speak in podcasts, videos, or live events. I would love to know what you're implementing or answer any questions you might have. Feel free to reach out on via Instagram or Facebook @cathyvchristen, or go to cathychristen.com and click on the contact tab to send me a message! I look forward to connecting with you and offering any value I can.

A QUICK FAVOR

If any of the concepts in this book helped you in any way, please share. Don't keep it all to yourself—we can make a bigger impact together! I am grateful to have been exposed to many of these concepts early on and will be forever grateful to the friend who gave me my first personal development book. Whose life can you forever impact?

Here are a few ways to help spread the impact:

- Write a review on Amazon
- Share your copy of this book with a friend
- Buy a copy for a friend

About the Author

CATHY CHRISTEN is a holistic peak performance strategist passionate about helping people design their life as the masterpiece it was meant to be. She brings awareness to the extraordinary potential within you, inspires you to fully develop the gifts you've been given, and provides business and personal coaching tools to help you elevate your energy to its highest level to start living the life of your dreams today!

She is a speaker, author, direct sales trainer, as well as a life and business strategist. She has coached over 100+ people over the past decade (including five national champions) to start and grow profitable businesses, and exclusively mentors thirty-five entrepreneurs annually across multiple market spaces. To have Cathy as a guest speaker (live or podcast) or to facilitate a transformational workshop, visit cathychristen.com.

Cathy is the founder and CEO of Elevated You, Inc. a coaching and consulting company focused on helping individuals and companies take their life and business to the next level. She oversees the Gulf Coast division of Cutco/Vector Marketing, which produces over $5.5 million in sales annually. She was the quickest promoted district manager to the Cutco Hall of Fame, won seven national titles, and is responsible for over $46 million dollars in sales. Cathy is also co-founder of Elevated Fitness and Nutrition, an energy and lifestyle company focused on a holistic approach to help others have the energy they need to really LIVE their best life.

Stay Connected with Cathy Christen

www.cathychristen.com

www.facebook.com/cathyvchristen

www.instagram.com/cathyvchristen

http://bit.ly/EFNcommunity

CPSIA information can be obtained
at www.ICGtesting.com
Printed in the USA
LVHW112340270519
619242LV00001B/60/P